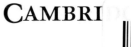

D0512142

UNL🔗CK

LISTENING & SPEAKING SKILLS

2

Stephanie Dimond-Bayir

CAMBRIDGE
UNIVERSITY PRESS

CAMBRIDGE
UNIVERSITY PRESS

University Printing House, Cambridge CB2 8BS, United Kingdom

Cambridge University Press is part of the University of Cambridge.

It furthers the University's mission by disseminating knowledge in the pursuit of education, learning and research at the highest international levels of excellence.

www.cambridge.org
Information on this title: www.cambridge.org/9781107682320

© Cambridge University Press 2014

First published 2014

Printed in China by Golden Cup Printing Co. Ltd

A catalogue record for this publication is available from the British Library

ISBN 978-1-107-68232-0 Listening and Speaking 2 Student's Book with Online Workbook
ISBN 978-1-107-64280-5 Listening and Speaking 2 Teacher's Book with DVD
ISBN 978-1-107-61400-0 Reading and Writing 2 Student's Book with Online Workbook
ISBN 978-1-107-61403-1 Reading and Writing 2 Teacher's Book with DVD

Additional resources for this publication at www.cambridge.org/unlock

Cambridge University Press has no responsibility for the persistence or accuracy of URLs for external or third-party internet websites referred to in this publication, and does not guarantee that any content on such websites is, or will remain, accurate or appropriate. Information regarding prices, travel timetables, and other factual information given in this work is correct at the time of first printing but Cambridge University Press does not guarantee the accuracy of such information thereafter.

CONTENTS

MAP OF THE BOOK

UNIT	VIDEO	LISTENING	VOCABULARY
1 PLACES Listening 1: A podcast about homes around the world (Geography) Listening 2: A lecture about satellite navigation systems (Travel management)	Living in Alaska	*Key listening skill*: Predicting content using visuals Listening for main ideas Listening for detail Understanding key vocabulary Distinguishing fact from opinion *Pronunciation for listening:* Vowel sounds: /eɪ/ /ɒ/ /ɪ/ /ʌ/	Vocabulary for places we live and work (*e.g. pedestrian area, bus stop, cottage*)
2 FESTIVALS AND CELEBRATIONS Listening 1: Three interviews about festivals in different countries (Social sciences) Listening 2: A talk about celebrations and food (Cultural studies)	A Chinese New Year	*Key listening skill*: Listening and taking notes Understanding key vocabulary Predicting content using visuals Listening for main ideas Listening for examples Recognizing examples *Pronunciation for listening:* Stressed words in connected speech	Collocations (*e.g. go to a concert, take a photograph, have a nice time*)
3 SCHOOL AND EDUCATION Listening 1: A guided tour of a university campus (University orientation) Listening 2: A discussion about learning with technology (Educational studies)	Education around the world	*Key listening skill*: Understanding key vocabulary Using visual clues to listen Activating your knowledge Listening for detail *Pronunciation for listening:* Word stress Understanding intonation	Collocations about learning (*e.g. study Geography, learn Biology, teach French, revise History*) Review of prepositional phrases
4 THE INTERNET AND TECHNOLOGY Listening 1: A student radio programme about robots (Sociology) Listening 2: A news report about how computers affect our memory (Psychology)	Virtual reality	*Key listening skill*: Understanding key vocabulary Listening for main ideas Listening for reasons Listening for additional details *Pronunciation for listening:* Consonant sounds: /s/ /ʃ/ /tʃ/ strong /æ/ and weak /ə/	Technology (*e.g. go online, wifi, the cloud*)
5 LANGUAGE AND COMMUNICATION Listening 1: Different genres of listening (English language and linguistics) Listening 2: Presentation about sign language (Sign language and deaf studies)	Languages in South America	*Key listening skill*: Using your knowledge to predict content Listening for genre Using your knowledge to predict content Understanding key vocabulary Listening for main ideas Listening for instructions *Pronunciation for listening:* Sounding positive Consonant sounds: silent /l/	Communication (*e.g. pick up, learn, wave*)

GRAMMAR	CRITICAL THINKING	SPEAKING
Review of the Past simple	Plan a presentation	**Preparation for speaking** Organize information for a presentation **Pronunciation for speaking** Connected speech **Speaking task** Create a presentation for your classmates about an interesting place. Give factual information about the place you choose.
Review of Present tense question forms	Use a table to organize ideas	**Preparation for speaking** Make suggestions **Speaking task** Discuss a new festival and make suggestions for events. Give a poster presentation about your festival to the rest of your group.
Basic verb patterns	Use an idea wheel to categorize vocabulary	**Preparation for speaking** Offer opinions, agree and disagree Phrases for giving opinions in a debate **Speaking task** Hold a debate about whether students should choose how they learn. Explain if you agree or disagree with your classmates during the debate.
can / be able to	Categorize advantages and disadvantages to hold a debate	**Preparation for speaking** Describe additional and contrasting information Linking words of contrast to organize a report **Speaking task** Present a report about technology, providing some information about a device. Look at advantages and disadvantages and details to support main ideas.
Imperative clauses Verb patterns	Use a flow chart to give instructions	**Preparation for speaking** Sequence instructions Sequencing words to organize instructions **Speaking task** Plan and give a set of instructions.

UNIT	VIDEO	LISTENING	VOCABULARY	
6 WEATHER AND CLIMATE Listening 1: A news report on the climate of the Western Ghats tropical rainforest (Geography) Listening 2: A discussion between two students who are preparing a survey about the weather and people's moods (Psychology and Social Sciences)	Rain and the water cycle	***Key listening skill:*** Understanding key vocabulary Predicting ideas from research Recognizing mood ***Pronunciation for listening:*** Vowel sounds: /ɒ/ /əʊ/ Sounding interested	Verb collocations	
7 SPORTS AND COMPETITION Listening 1: A panel discussion about the scoring system in Taekwondo (Sports science) Listening 2: A presentation about unusual sports (Sports science)	The Palio horse race	***Key listening skill:*** Understanding key vocabulary Listening for bias Listening for corrections ***Pronunciation for listening:*** Elision and weak forms Making corrections	Vocabulary for sport (*e.g. golf, gloves, rink*) Adverbs	
8 BUSINESS Listening 1: A conversation about wasting time at work (Business studies, Sociology) Listening 2: A discussion between a mentor and a student about interview techniques (Business studies)	South African Cape fishermen	***Key listening skill:*** Understanding key vocabulary Recognizing numbers Listening for reaction ***Pronunciation for listening:*** Pronouncing numbers	Multi-word verbs	
9 PEOPLE Listening 1: A conversation between two students about two remarkable people (History) Listening 2: A seminar discussion about inventions with unusual designs (Industrial design)	Internet inventors	***Key listening skill:*** Predicting content using visuals Understanding key vocabulary Listening for attitude Listening for detail ***Pronunciation for listening:*** Showing enthusiasm	*-ed* and *-ing* adjectives	
10 SPACE AND THE UNIVERSE Listening 1: A radio programme about space travel (Space studies) Listening 2: A discussion about the International Space Station (Space studies)	Exploring Mars	***Key listening skill:*** Understanding key vocabulary Using context to guess words Listening to an introduction ***Pronunciation for listening:*** Words with easily confused sounds Consonant sounds: /t/ /θ/	Travel verbs and nouns with similar meanings Word building	

GRAMMAR	CRITICAL THINKING	SPEAKING
Review of future forms	Use a consequence map	**Preparation for speaking** Linking words to explain cause and consequence **Speaking task** Create and complete a survey about the use of land and how it affects the climate. Present the results of the survey to your classmates.
Review of the Present perfect	Use ideas rakes	**Preparation for speaking** Phrases to talk about advantages and disadvantages, to explain that you don't understand and to ask for further explanation **Speaking task** Have a panel discussion about sport and money. Talk about advantages and disadvantages.
Review of comparatives	Use cluster diagrams	**Preparation for speaking** Phrases to give advice **Speaking task** Think of some solutions to a work or study problem and give advice to someone.
Suffixes	Use description wheels	**Preparation for speaking** Phrases and questions to talk about the appearance and functions of objects **Speaking task** Describe an object. Talk about what it looks like and its functions. Consider its advantages and disadvantages.
Conditionals	Use question charts	**Preparation for speaking** Using body language to show interest Phrases to invite others to speak, interrupt or continue speaking **Speaking task** Plan a conference about space exploration. Discuss and find solutions to any possible problems.

UNL♂CK UNIT STRUCTURE

The units in *Unlock Listening and Speaking Skills* are carefully scaffolded so that students build the skills and language they need throughout the unit in order to produce a successful Speaking task.

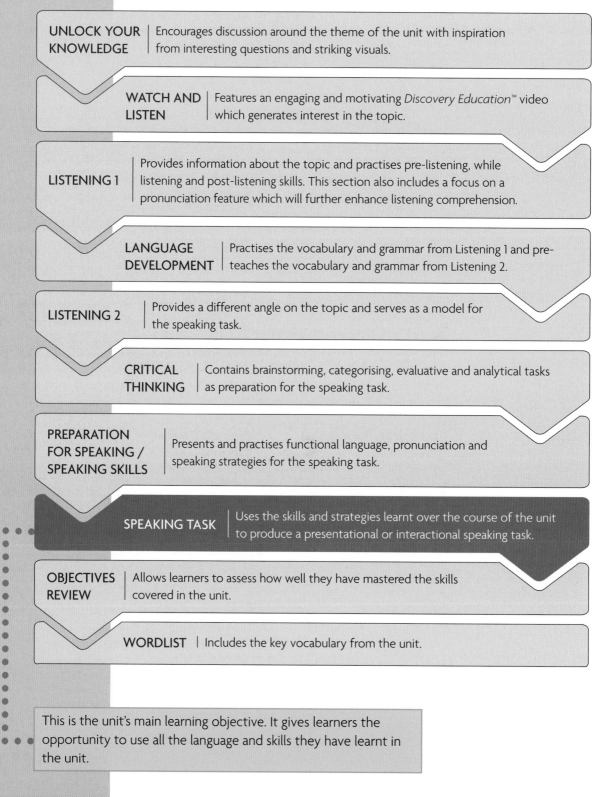

UNLOCK YOUR KNOWLEDGE | Encourages discussion around the theme of the unit with inspiration from interesting questions and striking visuals.

WATCH AND LISTEN | Features an engaging and motivating *Discovery Education*™ video which generates interest in the topic.

LISTENING 1 | Provides information about the topic and practises pre-listening, while listening and post-listening skills. This section also includes a focus on a pronunciation feature which will further enhance listening comprehension.

LANGUAGE DEVELOPMENT | Practises the vocabulary and grammar from Listening 1 and pre-teaches the vocabulary and grammar from Listening 2.

LISTENING 2 | Provides a different angle on the topic and serves as a model for the speaking task.

CRITICAL THINKING | Contains brainstorming, categorising, evaluative and analytical tasks as preparation for the speaking task.

PREPARATION FOR SPEAKING / SPEAKING SKILLS | Presents and practises functional language, pronunciation and speaking strategies for the speaking task.

SPEAKING TASK | Uses the skills and strategies learnt over the course of the unit to produce a presentational or interactional speaking task.

OBJECTIVES REVIEW | Allows learners to assess how well they have mastered the skills covered in the unit.

WORDLIST | Includes the key vocabulary from the unit.

This is the unit's main learning objective. It gives learners the opportunity to use all the language and skills they have learnt in the unit.

UNLØCK MOTIVATION

PERSONALIZE

Unlock encourages students to bring their own knowledge, experiences and opinions to the topics. This **motivates** students to relate the topics to their own contexts.

DISCOVERY EDUCATION™ VIDEO

Thought-provoking videos from *Discovery Education*™ are included in every unit throughout the course to introduce topics, promote discussion and motivate learners. The videos provide a new angle on a wide range of academic subjects.

> " The video was excellent! It helped with raising students' interest in the topic. It was well-structured and the language level was appropriate.
>
> Maria Agata Szczerbik,
> United Arab Emirates University,
> Al-Ain, UAE "

UNL⌀CK CRITICAL THINKING

> [...] with different styles of visual aids such as mind maps, grids, tables and pictures, this [critical thinking] section [provides] very crucial tools that can encourage learners to develop their speaking skills.
>
> Dr. Panidnad Chulerk, Rangit University, Thailand

BLOOM'S TAXONOMY

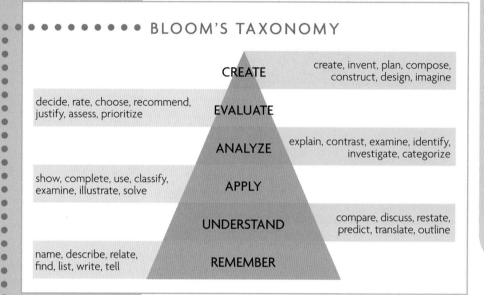

CREATE — create, invent, plan, compose, construct, design, imagine

decide, rate, choose, recommend, justify, assess, prioritize — EVALUATE

ANALYZE — explain, contrast, examine, identify, investigate, categorize

show, complete, use, classify, examine, illustrate, solve — APPLY

UNDERSTAND — compare, discuss, restate, predict, translate, outline

name, describe, relate, find, list, write, tell — REMEMBER

BLOOM'S TAXONOMY

The Critical thinking sections in *Unlock* are based on Benjamin Bloom's classification of learning objectives. This ensures learners develop their **lower-** and **higher-order thinking skills**, ranging from demonstrating **knowledge** and **understanding** to in-depth **evaluation**.

The margin headings in the Critical thinking sections highlight the exercises which develop Bloom's concepts.

LEARN TO THINK

Learners engage in **evaluative** and **analytical tasks** that are designed to ensure they do all of the thinking and information-gathering required for the end-of-unit speaking task.

CRITICAL THINKING

At the end of this unit you are going to do the speaking task below.

Plan and give a set of instructions.

Giving instructions

To give instructions, use a simple flow chart to help you think of the actions you will need to describe the process.

APPLY

2 Complete the instructions for setting the alarm on a mobile phone. Write the verbs in the box in the flow chart.

put   enter   save   pick   unlock   select   press

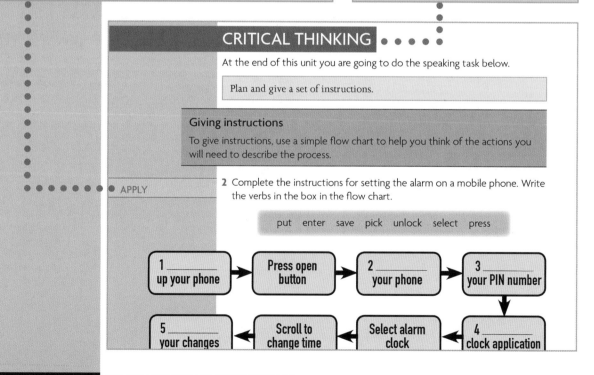

1 _____ up your phone → Press open button → 2 _____ your phone → 3 _____ your PIN number ↓

5 _____ your changes ← Scroll to change time ← Select alarm clock ← 4 _____ clock application

UNL CK RESEARCH

THE CAMBRIDGE LEARNER CORPUS 👁

The **Cambridge Learner Corpus** is a bank of official Cambridge English exam papers. Our exclusive access means we can use the corpus to carry out unique research and identify the most common errors that learners make. That information is used to ensure the *Unlock* syllabus teaches the most **relevant language**.

THE WORDS YOU NEED

Language Development sections provide vocabulary and grammar-building tasks that are further practised in the 👁 **UNL CK ONLINE** Workbook. The glossary provides definitions and pronunciation, and the end-of-unit wordlists provide useful summaries of key vocabulary.

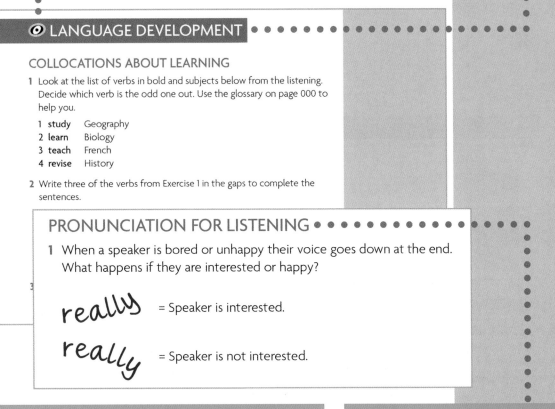

👁 LANGUAGE DEVELOPMENT

COLLOCATIONS ABOUT LEARNING

1 Look at the list of verbs in bold and subjects below from the listening. Decide which verb is the odd one out. Use the glossary on page 000 to help you.

1 **study**   Geography
2 **learn**   Biology
3 **teach**   French
4 **revise** History

2 Write three of the verbs from Exercise 1 in the gaps to complete the sentences.

PRONUNCIATION FOR LISTENING

1 When a speaker is bored or unhappy their voice goes down at the end. What happens if they are interested or happy?

really = Speaker is interested.

really = Speaker is not interested.

ACADEMIC LANGUAGE

Unique research using the **Cambridge English Corpus** has been carried out into academic language, in order to provide learners with relevant, academic vocabulary from the start (CEFR A1 and above). This addresses a gap in current academic vocabulary mapping and ensures learners are presented with carefully selected words which they will find essential during their studies.

PRONUNCIATION FOR LISTENING

This unique feature of *Unlock* focuses on aspects of pronunciation which may inhibit listening comprehension. This means that learners are primed to understand detail and nuance while listening.

> " The language development is clear and the strong lexical focus is positive as learners feel they make more progress when they learn more vocabulary.
>
> Colleen Wackrow,
> Princess Nourah Bint Abdulrahman University, Al-Riyadh, Kingdom of Saudi Arabia "

UNL😮CK SOLUTIONS

FLEXIBLE

Unlock is available in a range of print and digital components, so teachers can mix and match according to their requirements.

UNL😮CK ONLINE WORKBOOKS

The **UNL😮CK ONLINE** Workbooks are accessed via activation codes packaged with the Student's Books. These **easy-to-use** workbooks provide interactive exercises, games, tasks, and further practice of the language and skills from the Student's Books in the Cambridge LMS, an engaging and modern learning environment.

CAMBRIDGE LEARNING MANAGEMENT SYSTEM (LMS)

The Cambridge LMS provides teachers with the ability to track learner progress and save valuable time thanks to automated marking functionality. Blogs, forums and other tools are also available to facilitate communication between students and teachers.

UNL😮CK EBOOKS

The *Unlock* Student's Books and Teacher's Books are also available as interactive eBooks. With answers and *Discovery Education*™ videos embedded, the eBooks provide a great alternative to the printed materials.

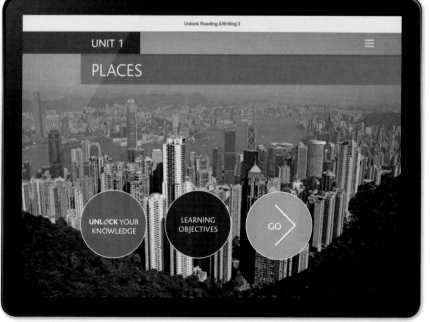

COURSE COMPONENTS

- Each level of *Unlock* consists of two Student's Books: **Reading & Writing** and **Listening & Speaking** and an accompanying Teacher's Book for each. Online Workbooks are packaged with each Student's Book.
- Complete course audio is available to download from www.cambridge.org/unlock
- Look out for the **UNL♂CK ONLINE** symbols in the Student's Books which indicate that additional practice of that skill or language area is available in the Online Workbook.
- Every *Unlock* Student's Book is delivered both in print format and as an interactive **eBook for tablet devices**.
- The *Unlock* Teacher's Books contain additional speaking tasks, tests, teaching tips and research projects for students.
- *Presentation Plus* **software for interactive whiteboards** is available for all Student's Books.

LISTENING AND SPEAKING

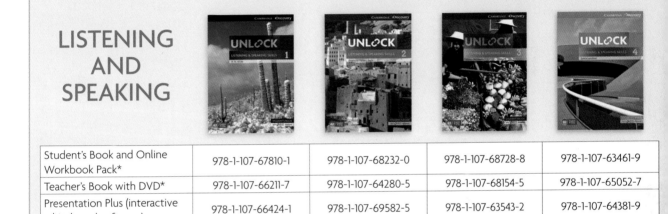

Student's Book and Online Workbook Pack*	978-1-107-67810-1	978-1-107-68232-0	978-1-107-68728-8	978-1-107-63461-9
Teacher's Book with DVD*	978-1-107-66211-7	978-1-107-64280-5	978-1-107-68154-5	978-1-107-65052-7
Presentation Plus (interactive whiteboard software)	978-1-107-66424-1	978-1-107-69582-5	978-1-107-63543-2	978-1-107-64381-9

*eBooks available from **www.cambridge.org/unlock**

The complete course audio is available from
www.cambridge.org/unlock

READING AND WRITING

Student's Book and Online Workbook Pack*	978-1-107-61399-7	978-1-107-61400-0	978-1-107-61526-7	978-1-107-61525-0
Teacher's Book with DVD*	978-1-107-61401-7	978-1-107-61403-1	978-1-107-61404-8	978-1-107-61409-3
Presentation Plus (interactive whiteboard software)	978-1-107-63800-6	978-1-107-65605-5	978-1-107-67624-4	978-1-107-68245-0

*eBooks available from **www.cambridge.org/unlock**

LEARNING OBJECTIVES

Watch and listen	Watch and understand a film about living in Alaska
Listening skills	Predict content using visuals; listen for fact and opinion
Speaking skills	Organize information for a presentation
Speaking task	Give a presentation about an interesting place

UNL⊘CK YOUR KNOWLEDGE

Work in pairs. Look at the photograph and answer the questions.

1 Would you prefer to live in a house or a block of flats? Why?
2 Do you think the flats in the photograph are unusual? Why?
3 Why do people choose to live in unusual places?
4 Which place would you prefer to live: by the sea, on a mountain or in a city centre? Why?

WATCH AND LISTEN

PREPARING TO WATCH

UNDERSTANDING
KEY VOCABULARY

1 Match the verbs (1–8) to the phrases (a–h).

1 chop	a the house
2 live	b wood into a stove
3 store	c cattle home
4 heat	d wood
5 prepare	e from the land
6 collect	f vegetables from the garden
7 drive	g wood and food safely
8 put	h the home for winter

2 Why is it difficult to live in Alaska? Write down three ideas.

WHILE WATCHING

LISTENING FOR KEY
INFORMATION

3 ▶ Watch the video and check your answers to Exercise 2.

4 ▶ Look at the photographs of jobs the Kilcher family do before winter. Watch the video again from 01:25. Number the photographs in the order you see them.

UNL☺CK LISTENING AND SPEAKING SKILLS 2

5 Work in pairs. Describe what is happening in each photograph. Use the verb phrases from Exercise 1.

6 Match each question (1–6) to an answer (a–f).

Why:

1 is the winter hard?
2 do people live from the land and grow food?
3 do the Kilchers chop wood and keep it near the house?
4 is the chopped wood important?
5 do the Kilchers drive the cattle from Kachemak Bay?
6 do they store vegetables in boxes?

a It keeps them safe for winter.
b It is used for fuel to heat the house for the whole of the winter.
c There are no shops or supermarkets close by.
d They want to keep them at home while the weather is bad.
e It lasts for eight months and the temperature can be -60°C.
f There is too much snow to move it all later.

7 ▶ Watch again. Check your answers.

DISCUSSION

8 Work in pairs and answer the questions.

1 Would you like to live in Alaska for one winter? Why / why not?
2 Do you think the lifestyle in Alaska is healthy?
3 Which problems do people living in cities have?

9 Work in groups of four. You are going to live in Alaska next winter. You can take three things with you to make life comfortable. Follow the instructions.

1 Work on your own. Write down three things you would like to take to Alaska.
   a phone, a TV ....
2 Discuss your items with your group. Choose three things for the whole group.
3 Find someone from another group. Tell them which three things you are taking and why.

PREPARING TO LISTEN

**UNLOCK
ONLINE**

Predicting key words and activating knowledge

Before you listen, look quickly at any pictures. Think of important or 'key' words to describe the pictures. Doing this helps you understand more when you listen. If you know the key words you can understand the main ideas and follow the information. Remember you don't need to understand every word.

PREDICTING
CONTENT USING
VISUALS

1 You are going to listen to a podcast about homes around the world. Match the words in the box to the photographs above. Use the glossary on page 199 to help you.

> cave   mushroom-shaped   ancient
> bridge   industrial   rock

**UNLOCK
ONLINE**

2 Look at the questions below. Match the words in italics with their definitions (a–c).

1 Do you *recognize* any of the places? Where do you think they are?
2 Which do you think are *strange*?
3 Which one is *located* next to the sea?

a different from normal
b know something or someone because you have seen it before
c to be in or near a place

3 Work in pairs. Answer the questions in Exercise 2 for the photographs above.

PRONUNCIATION FOR LISTENING

4 🔊**11** Listen to each word in the table.

/eɪ/	/ɒ/	/ɪ/	/ʌ/
pl<u>a</u>ce	h<u>o</u>t	q<u>ui</u>ck	<u>u</u>p
_____	_____	_____	_____
_____	_____	_____	_____
_____			

5 Work in pairs. Say the words from Exercise 4 with your partner and notice the underlined sound. Write the words from Exercise 1 in the table in Exercise 4.

6 Write the words below in the table in Exercise 4.

> beaut<u>i</u>ful   l<u>o</u>ng   str<u>a</u>nge   l<u>o</u>vely

7 Work with a partner. Take it in turns to read a word from lists A–D out loud. Your partner should listen carefully and tell you which word you have said.

Student A: 'cut' Student B: 'You said cut. Number 2. List D.'

	A	B	C	D
1	hate	hot	hit	hut
2	Kate	cot	kit	cut

WHILE LISTENING

8 🔊**12** Look at the questions below. Listen and choose the correct option.

1 The speakers on the podcast are:
   a politicians.
   b lecturers.
   c travel presenters.

2 The main topic of the podcast is:
   a travelling to different countries.
   b unusual places where people live.
   c a history of ancient houses.

LISTENING FOR
MAIN IDEAS

9 Circle the correct answers in these sentences about the gapped answers in the table in Exercise 10.

1 The words in the gaps in Column A will probably be *names / numbers / adjectives*.

2 The words in the gaps in Column B will probably be *names / numbers / adjectives*.

3 Each time you hear the name of *a place / person*, you can listen for the *names / numbers* that follow. This will help you listen at the right time.

10 🔊 **12** Listen to the podcast again. Write a word in the gaps to complete the table.

A country	B information
Matmata is in 1 _____ .	Matmata is 2 _____ years old. 3 It is located _____ kilometres south of Tunis.
Cappadocia is in 4 _____ .	The caves formed about 5 _____ years ago.
Ponte Vecchio is in 6 _____ .	It was built in 7 _____ .
Neft Dashlari is in 8 _____ .	The bridge is 9 _____ miles long. 10 _____ people live there.

DISCUSSION

11 Choose one of the questions below to talk about.

1 What is the most interesting building you know?

2 Can you describe your own house or flat?

3 Are there any differences in how people live in different parts of your country?

12 Work with a partner who has chosen a different question. Take turns to tell your partner the answer to the question you have chosen. Ask follow-up questions.

⊘ LANGUAGE DEVELOPMENT

REVIEW OF THE PAST SIMPLE

1 Circle the verbs in the Past simple in the sentences from Listening 1.

> 1 People started living in them 700 years ago.
>
> 2 … I went to Cappadocia in Turkey.
>
> 3 But did you know some people live on bridges?
>
> 4 People changed them into homes during the Roman period.
>
> 5 There was another bridge there before but an accident destroyed it.
>
> 6 They decided that the workers needed somewhere to live so they built a kind of 'city' above the sea.
>
> 7 They put houses, libraries, schools and even a cinema there.

2 Answer the questions about the sentences in Exercise 1.

   1 Which example is a question? Which auxiliary verb is used?
   2 When we ask a question, is the main verb in the past or in the infinitive form?

3 Complete the table with the main verbs from Exercise 1.

Past simple verbs: regular (add –ed)	Past simple verbs: irregular
started	
	knew

4 Write the correct verb in the gaps to complete the questions.

   1 When _____ (you / start) to live in your house?
   2 Where _____ (be) your mother's house when she was a child?
   3 Where _____ (you / go) on your last holiday?
   4 _____ (you / know) the people who lived near you when you were a child?
   5 How often _____ (you / change) the colour of your bedroom walls when you were young?

5 Work in pairs. Choose two of the questions to ask your partner. Take turns to ask and answer.

PLACES WHERE WE LIVE AND WORK

6 In Neft Dashlari there are houses, libraries, schools and even a cinema. Would you usually see these things in a town or in the countryside?

7 Label pictures a–l with the words in the box. Use the glossary on pages 199–200 to help you.

> forest   traffic lights   wildlife   bus stop   coffee shop   mountain
> tourist information office   cottage   field   lake   river   street

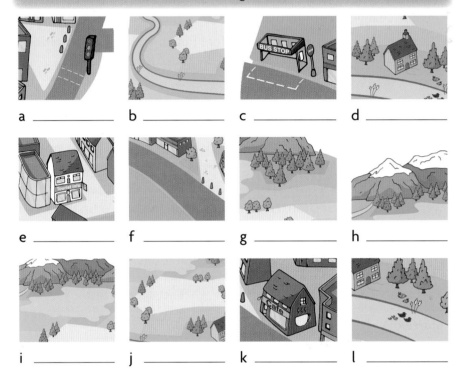

a _____   b _____   c _____   d _____

e _____   f _____   g _____   h _____

i _____   j _____   k _____   l _____

8 Use the pictures above to help you answer the questions.

1 Which places in the town can you wait at and why?
2 What can you cross in the town and in the country?
3 Which place can you get information from?
4 Where could you have a break and relax?
5 Is there anything in the pictures not found in your country?

9 Work with a partner. Choose five of the words or objects in the pictures. Describe the word you have chosen in one sentence. Can your partner guess the word?

A: It crosses a river or a road
B: Is it a bridge?

10 Work in small groups and tell each other:

- Your favourite place to have a break
- A place where you meet friends
- A place you work or study

LISTENING 2

PREPARING TO LISTEN

1 Look at the vocabulary in the word cloud. You are going to listen to a teacher giving a lecture. What do you think it is about?

UNDERSTANDING
KEY VOCABULARY

process
method
Satnav
believe
feel
area
GPS
tour
clear
obviously
route
complicated

2 Match the sentence halves. Use the glossary on pages 199–200 to help you.

1 When we *process* information
2 Something difficult to understand
3 I say *obviously* or *it is clear*
4 If I *personally feel*, *think* or *believe* something

a is *complicated* or *complex*.
b when I give a *fact* everyone knows.
c we organize and understand it.
d it is my *opinion*.

WHILE LISTENING

3 🔊 1.3 Listen to the lecture and check your answers to Exercise 1. Was the lecture about:

a how to use a satnav / GPS to find your way?
b the advantages and disadvantages of a satnav / GPS?
c different uses of technology in cars?

LISTENING FOR GIST

navigation time
stress -trafic/

UNLOCK
ONLINE

4 Read the sentences. Write *F* if the sentence is a fact. Write *O* if it is the opinion of the speaker. Write *DK* if we don't know.

1 Satnavs are usually in new cars. _F_
2 Satnavs were first made in 1978. _F_
3 Satnavs are more useful than phones when you want to find your way. _O_
4 It is difficult to read a map when driving. _F_
5 Satnavs can tell us if the traffic is good or bad. _F_
6 The brain takes time to process the pictures on a satnav. _F_
7 Satnavs can cause accidents. _F_ ✓
8 Most drivers listen to the satnav and don't always look. _O_

5 🔊 **1.3** Listen again. Check your answers.

POST-LISTENING

6 Read the audioscript on page 210 and write phrases that introduce opinions and facts in the gaps to complete the sentences.

1 Who has a satnav? ... So that is most of us. _____ , satnavs are now in most new cars.
2 As _we know_ , they give us directions while we drive and we can also look at the photographs or images.
3 Some scientists _have found_ that satnavs can be dangerous.
4 Now, _I think_ that this may be true.
5 But I also _believe_ that our journeys are more complicated.
6 ... this might cause accidents. And I _personally feel_ that most drivers listen to a satnav.
7 In _my opinion_ , the photographs on the satnav are not important.
8 It _seems to me_ that drivers don't actually look at the satnav very often.

7 Which phrases introduce opinions and which introduce facts? Which tense is often used to give facts?

8 The phrases from Listening 2, Exercise 6 tell us if the information is factual or the opinion of the speaker. Add the phrases to the grouping diagrams below.

FACT

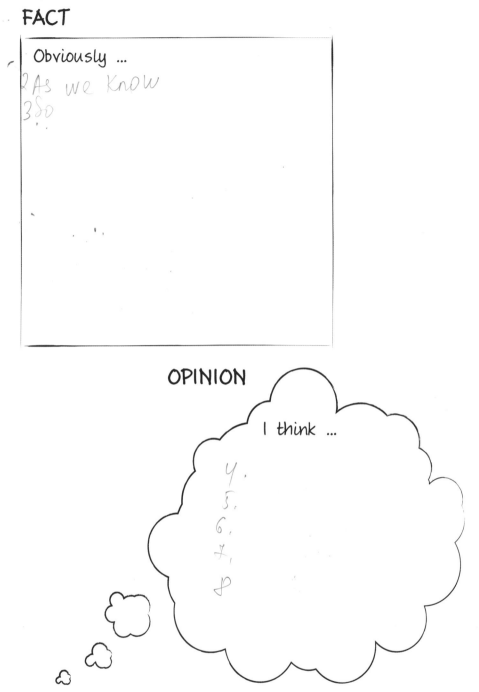

Obviously ...

2 As we know

3 So

OPINION

I think ...

4.

5.

6.

7.

8

DISCUSSION

9 Work in pairs. Discuss whether you use a satnav or a map in a car or on your phone when going to new places. Which do you prefer and why?

CRITICAL THINKING

At the end of this unit you are going to do the speaking task below.

> Create a presentation for your classmates about an interesting place. Present factual information and give your opinion about the place you choose.

1 Work with a partner and describe your homes to each other. Give two facts and two opinions.

My house has three bedrooms. Two are blue and the other is white. I think my house is very comfortable and beautiful.

2 Label the places from Listening 1 with three facts from categories 1–3.

1 the place it is located
2 reason why it is unusual
3 age

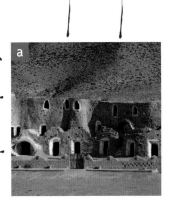

beautiful small

Age: Built 1300s/historic

Location: Florence, Italy

Unusual: has shops

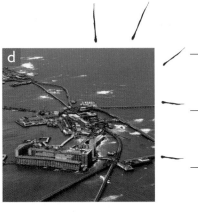

3 Use a different colour and add two opinions to the places from
Listening 1. Think about:

1 what the place looks like
2 what it is like to live there

Planning a presentation

Use a table to plan your presentation so that it is well-organized and you have
enough to say. Add sections for an introduction, general facts about your topic,
advantages, disadvantages as well as a summary.

4 Imagine you are going to present one of the places in Exercise 2 to your
class. Make a list of ideas to include in your presentation.

5 Now look at the table below. Did you include the same things in your list?

6 Write a heading from the box in the gaps to complete Column A of
the table.

> opinion (disadvantages)   ~~summary~~   opinion (advantages)
> introduction & general facts   history

A plan for presentation	B information in each part of presentation
1 _____ Name of place / country / location	
2 _____ How old? Who made it / other events?	
3 _____ Interesting / beautiful? Why visit?	
4 _____ Expensive / too crowded? Problems?	
5 SUMMARY Good? Go or not?	

7 Choose one of the places from Exercise 2. Write notes in column B of the
table.

8 Work with a partner. Using your notes, take turns to tell each other about
the place you have chosen. Don't say the name of the place. Your partner
should listen and guess the place you chose.

SPEAKING

PREPARATION FOR SPEAKING

1 When you present information it is important to organize what you say into different topics. Match topics 1–4 to sentences a–d.

1 General fact	a	Satnavs are good when you are going to a new place.
2 Advantages		
3 Disadvantages	b	Satnavs can stop drivers thinking about the road.
4 Summary	c	Satnavs have more advantages than disadvantages.
	d	Satnavs were first made in 1978 to help drivers find their way.

2 🔊 **1.4** To help you prepare for your presentation, here is some language that you can use. Listen and circle the organizing phrase that you hear.

1 *I'd like to talk about / I'd like to tell you about* the advantages and disadvantages of satnavs.
2 *First of all / Firstly*, let's look at the advantages.
3 *I'd also like to talk about / I'd also like to give you* some disadvantages.
4 *In summary / Finally*, the advantages of satnavs, in my opinion are greater than the disadvantages.

PRONUNCIATION FOR SPEAKING

3 🔊 **1.5** Look at the organizing phrases again and listen to the first example. Notice that the words *talk about* are connected.

I'd like to talk‿about the advantages and disadvantages of satnavs.

4 Look at the last letter of the word *talk* and the first letter of *about*. Complete the rule by circling the correct word.

When one word ends in a (consonant) / *vowel* sound and the next begins with a *consonant* / (vowel) sound, there is a link between them: *talk‿about* becomes /tɔːkəbaʊt/

5 Draw the three links between the consonants and vowels in the phrase.

First of all, let's look at the advantages.

6 🔊 **1.6** Listen and repeat the phrase.

7 Work with a partner. Mark the links in the following phrases. Then take turns to say the phrases.

1 I'd like to give some information about ...
2 Now let's talk about ...
3 The next topic is ...
4 Finally let's look at ...

8 Student A, turn to page 194 and follow the instructions. Student B, turn to page 196 and follow the instructions.

Student A, turn to page 194 and follow the instructions. Student B, turn to page 196 and follow the instructions.

ORGANIZING INFORMATION FOR A PRESENTATION

SPEAKING TASK

> Create a presentation for your classmates about an interesting place. Present factual information and give your opinion about the place you choose.

PREPARE

1 Choose an unusual or interesting place you know. Try to think of somewhere other people might not know.

2 Find out some facts about the place you have chosen and note down your own ideas / opinions of the place.

3 Write an outline plan for the presentation. Use the table below to help you to organize your presentation.

A plan for presentation	B information in each part of presentation
introduction Name of place	
history How old? Who made it / other events?	
opinion: advantages Interesting / beautiful? Why visit?	
opinion: disadvantages Expensive / too crowded? Problems?	
summary Good? Go or not?	

PRESENT

4 Work in groups of three or four. Present your information to each other. While listening, you can ask questions about what you hear.

5 Vote for the place that most students would like to visit.

TASK CHECKLIST	✔
Have you used the Past simple correctly?	
Have you organized your presentation using appropriate organizing phrases?	
Have you introduced facts and opinions using the correct language?	
Have you joined sounds in phrases when the words link together?	

OBJECTIVES REVIEW

I can ...

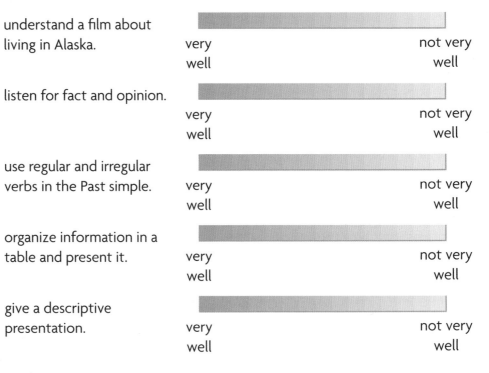

understand a film about living in Alaska.

very well   not very well

listen for fact and opinion.

very well   not very well

use regular and irregular verbs in the Past simple.

very well   not very well

organize information in a table and present it.

very well   not very well

give a descriptive presentation.

very well   not very well

WORDLIST

UNIT VOCABULARY	
advantages (n)	long (adj)
ancient (adj)	lovely (adj)
area (n)	method (n)
beautiful (adj)	mountain (n)
believe (v)	mushroom-shaped (adj)
bridge (n)	obviously (adv)
bus stop (n)	opinion (n)
castle (n)	pedestrian area (n)
cave (n)	personally (adv)
clear (adj)	process (n)
coffee shop (n)	recognize (v)
complex (adj)	river (n)
complicated (adj)	rock (n)
cottage (n)	route (n)
crossroads (n)	satnav (n)
dangerous (adj)	strange (adj)
desert (n)	street (n)
fact (n)	summary (n)
feel (v)	think (v)
field (n)	tour (n)
finally (adv)	tourist information office (n)
firstly (adv)	traffic lights (n)
forest (n)	trip (n)
industrial (adj)	unusual (adj)
journey (n)	way (n)
lake (n)	wildlife (n)
located (v)	

LEARNING OBJECTIVES

Watch and listen	Watch and understand a video about New Year in China
Listening skills	Listen and take notes; listen for main ideas
Speaking skills	Make suggestions
Speaking task	Give a poster presentation about a festival

UNLOCK YOUR KNOWLEDGE

Work in pairs. Look at the photograph and answer the questions.

1 Which country do you think the festival is held in?
2 Are there any public festivals in your country which use colour?
3 A public festival is for everyone but a private celebration is only for family and friends. What kinds of festivals and celebrations have you been to?

PREPARING TO WATCH

UNDERSTANDING
KEY VOCABULARY

1 Match the words (1–6) to the photographs (a–f).

1 envelopes d
2 fireworks f
3 banners b
4 lanterns a
5 costume e
6 parade c

2 Write the verbs from the box in the gaps to complete the sentences.

> paint   exchange   celebrate   decorate
> welcomed   travel   wear

1 All around the world, people _celebrate_ festivals.
2 800 million people _travel_ across China to be with their friends and family.
3 People _decorate_ their homes with red lanterns.
4 They _paint_ red paper banners.
5 People _wear_ bright costumes.
6 They _exchange_ gifts of money.
7 The New Year is _welcomed_ with fireworks.

WHILE WATCHING

3 ▶ Watch the video and check your answers to Exercise 2.

4 ▶ Watch again. Circle the correct answers to the questions below.

1 How long is the Chinese New Year Festival? *12 / 15* days
2 When is the Chinese New Year? *spring / winter*
3 What words do people paint on the banners? *happiness and wealth / good luck and wealth*
4 Where do people hang these banners? *inside the house / outside the house*
5 Who carries the dragon in a dragon dance? *men / women*
6 The family meal on New Year has *15 / 22* courses.
7 What do people put gifts of money in? *red bags / red envelopes*
8 What things do people give to their friends as gifts? *sweets / apples*
9 How many people come to see fireworks in Hong Kong? *1 / 3* million

UNDERSTANDING
MAIN IDEAS

LISTENING FOR KEY
INFORMATION

DISCUSSION

5 Work with a partner. Discuss the questions below.

1 Would you like to visit China for New Year? Why / Why not?
2 How do you celebrate New Year?

PREPARING TO LISTEN

UNDERSTANDING KEY VOCABULARY

1 You are going to listen to some information about three festivals. You will hear the words in bold below. Choose the correct option to complete the definitions. Use the glossary on page 200 to help you.

1 A **lecture** is a *book / talk* given by a teacher or professor.
2 An **activity** is *something organized for enjoyment / an exam or test.*
3 **Traditional** activities *have been done for a long time / are new* in a particular country.
4 If a festival is about **culture**, it usually shows the *customs, art, music and food / work and business* of a country.
5 A **band** is a *type of music / group of musicians.*
6 A **camel** is a large animal usually found in the *jungle / desert.*
7 If something is **entertainment**, we do it so that we *can enjoy it / learn from it.*

2 Match the words in bold in Exercise 1 to the photographs (a–c). Some words can be matched to more than one photograph.

PREDICTING CONTENT USING VISUALS

3 Match the festivals (1–3) with the photographs (a–c).

1 The Cambridge Festival of Ideas — c
2 The Muscat Festival of Heritage and Culture b
3 Iceland Airwaves Music Festival — a

WHILE LISTENING

LISTENING AND TAKING NOTES

UNLOCK ONLINE

4 🔊 2.1 Listen and check your answers to Exercise 3.

5 Cross out the words that are not needed in the notes.

1 Date: the festival is in April and May.
2 Activities: you can see art and you can try cooking.

Listening and taking notes

Remember that notes should be short. If you write too much you sometimes miss the next part of the listening. Only write the most important words.

> Place: ~~the festival is in~~ Muscat

6 Look at the tourist information brochure advertising the three different festivals. Predict the type of information in each gap.

7 🔊 **2.1** Listen again and check your predictions.

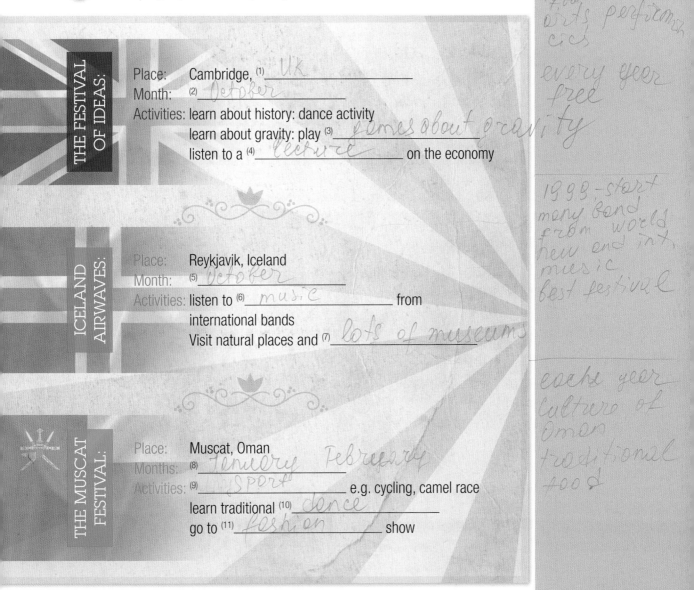

THE FESTIVAL OF IDEAS:

Place: Cambridge, (1) _UK_
Month: (2) _October_
Activities: learn about history: dance activity
learn about gravity: play (3) _games about gravity_
listen to a (4) _lecture_ on the economy

ICELAND AIRWAVES:

Place: Reykjavik, Iceland
Month: (5) _October_
Activities: listen to (6) _music_ from international bands
Visit natural places and (7) _lots of museums_

THE MUSCAT FESTIVAL:

Place: Muscat, Oman
Months: (8) _January February_
Activities: (9) _Sport_ e.g. cycling, camel race
learn traditional (10) _dance_
go to (11) _fashion_ show

Handwritten margin notes:

2005 14 no
7.000 arts performances
every year
free

1998 - start
many band
from world
new and int.
music
best festival

each year
culture of
Oman
traditional
food

DISCUSSION

8 Think about a festival in your country. Make some notes on what you can do at the festival. Decide which activities you like / would like to do most.

9 Speak to at least three other people in the class. Tell them about the festival you have chosen. Find out which activities they would like to do at your festival.

10 Compare answers with the rest of the class. Which festivals and activities are most popular?

PRONUNCIATION FOR LISTENING

11 Look at the following sentence from Listening 1. Which words are important to understand the sentence? Underline them.

> It is an interesting event to come to.

UNLOCK ONLINE

12 🔊 2.2 Now listen to the sentence. Which words are stressed?

13 Look at the following questions from the listening. Underline the words that are stressed.

1 ... what kind of things do people do?
2 Are there any things you don't like ... ?
3 Have you got many people here from other countries?

14 🔊 2.3 Listen and check. Repeat the phrases.

15 Write some questions for your partner about their free time. Use the sentence stems below to help you.

1 What / activities / do / you / do / free time?
2 Have / you / got / hobbies?
3 Can / you / describe / last weekend?

16 Underline the important words in the questions.

17 Work with a partner. Ask and answer the questions.

⊙ LANGUAGE DEVELOPMENT

REVIEW OF PRESENT TENSE QUESTION FORMS

1 The questions (1–3) from Listening 1 are in the present tense. Underline the main verb in each one. Which one is in the Present continuous?

> 1 So what kind of things do people learn?
>
> 2 Are you ever bored?
>
> 3 Are you enjoying the festival?

2 Two of the rules (1–5) in the box are incorrect. Read and correct the rules.

EXPLANATION

1 Present simple is used to talk about habits, routines and facts.

2 Present continuous is used to talk about actions happening now.

3 The auxiliary verbs used with Present simple are: *am / is / are* and the verb + -*ing*. ——

4 The auxiliary verbs used with the question form of the Present continuous are: *do / does.* are

5 When there is a noun or adjective in Present simple questions, questions can be made with a form of *be* (*am / is /are*).

6 Use *do* or *does* in sentences with a main verb in the Present simple.

Do you like music?
Does he play the guitar?
✗ Are you like music This is incorrect because *like* is Present simple.

7 Use *are* or *is* in sentences with a main verb in the -*ing* form.

Are you listening to pop music?

8 Use *are* or *is* in sentences with adjectives or nouns.

Are you good at music?
Are you musical?
✗ Do you listening to music This is incorrect because *listening* has -*ing*.
✗ Do you a musician This is incorrect because *musician* is a noun.

3 A presenter on a radio programme is going to interview the organizer of a food festival. Read the interview questions and correct the errors in the auxiliary verbs in questions 1–8.

1 <u>Are</u> you like your job?
2 <u>Do</u> you a chef?
3 What time <u>is</u> the festival start?
4 What kinds of food <u>are</u> you have?
5 <u>Does</u> it all good?
6 Where <u>are</u> people eat their lunch?
7 <u>Does</u> the people coming here to buy food or eat it?
8 <u>Do</u> the work interesting?

4 🔊 **2.4** Listen and check your answers to Exercise 4.

5 Use the words to make questions in the Present tense.

1 you / like / fish and meat?
2 other people like / your food?
3 you / a good cook?
4 you / feel / hungry now?

6 Work with a partner. Ask each other the questions.

COLLOCATIONS

A collocation is a combination of two or more words which are used together in a way that sounds correct.

e.g. go to University, go to a talk, go to class

7 Label each circle with the correct word from the box to make verb +
noun collocations. Some words can be used more than once.

> a photograph   a test (x2)   a celebration (x2)
> a concert   an exam (x3)   a festival   a lecture (x2)
> a party (x2)   advice   care   fun   a problem
> a nice time   notes   school   university   your time

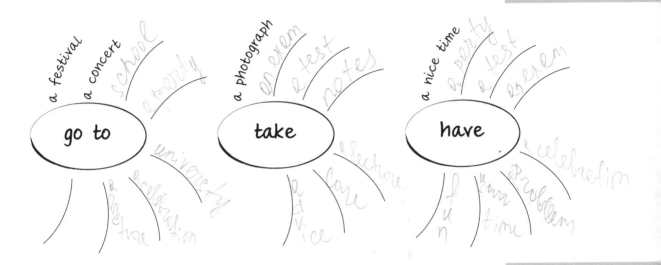

8 Write the correct form of *go, have* or *take* in the gaps to complete the
sentences.

1 Excuse me, can you ___take___ a photograph of me and my sister?

2 What time do you leave your house to ___go___ to school?

3 I'm going on holiday next week. Will you ___take___ care of my plants?

4 ___Have___ a nice time when you go on holiday!

5 I can't go to class today. Will you ___take___ notes for me?

9 Write the correct form of the words in Exercise 7 in the gaps to complete
the questions. More than one answer may be possible.

1 What do you think makes a good student? Do good students always go
to ___a lecture___ or do they miss them?

2 When you take ___a test___ do you usually pass?

3 How old are people when they go to ___university___ and study for a
degree in your country?

4 Who do you usually take advice from if you have a ___problem___ ?

5 If it is your birthday do you have a ___party___ ?

10 Work with a partner. Ask and answer the questions.

LISTENING 2

PREPARING TO LISTEN

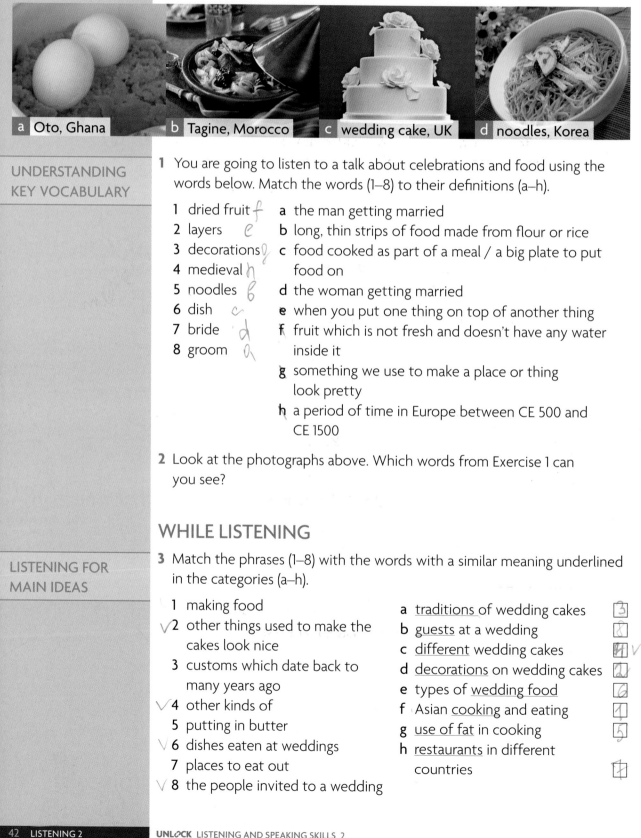

a Oto, Ghana | b Tagine, Morocco | c wedding cake, UK | d noodles, Korea

UNDERSTANDING
KEY VOCABULARY

1 You are going to listen to a talk about celebrations and food using the words below. Match the words (1–8) to their definitions (a–h).

1 dried fruit *f*   a the man getting married
2 layers *e*   b long, thin strips of food made from flour or rice
3 decorations *g*   c food cooked as part of a meal / a big plate to put food on
4 medieval *h*
5 noodles *b*   d the woman getting married
6 dish *c*   e when you put one thing on top of another thing
7 bride *d*   f fruit which is not fresh and doesn't have any water inside it
8 groom *a*
   g something we use to make a place or thing look pretty
   h a period of time in Europe between CE 500 and CE 1500

2 Look at the photographs above. Which words from Exercise 1 can you see?

WHILE LISTENING

LISTENING FOR
MAIN IDEAS

3 Match the phrases (1–8) with the words with a similar meaning underlined in the categories (a–h).

1 making food
✓2 other things used to make the cakes look nice
3 customs which date back to many years ago
✓4 other kinds of
5 putting in butter
✓6 dishes eaten at weddings
7 places to eat out
✓8 the people invited to a wedding

a traditions of wedding cakes   3
b guests at a wedding   8
c different wedding cakes   4 ✓
d decorations on wedding cakes   2
e types of wedding food   6
f Asian cooking and eating   1
g use of fat in cooking   5
h restaurants in different countries   7

UNL⊘CK LISTENING AND SPEAKING SKILLS 2

4 🔊 **2.5** Listen and tick the categories (a–h) in Exercise 3 you hear about.

5 🔊 **2.5** Listen again. Match the country (1–5) to the wedding food (a–e).

1 Australia *e*
2 Bermuda *a*
3 Korea *d*
4 Ghana *c*
5 Morocco *b*

a two cakes
b tagine: meat in sauce
c oto: yam and eggs
d kuk so: long noodles
e white wedding cake

POST-LISTENING

6 🔊 **2.6** Listen to the examples of food at different weddings. Write phrases for introducing examples in the gaps to complete the sentences.

1 ... nowadays some people prefer different kinds, *such as* chocolate.
2 Most traditional Western cakes have three or four layers with beautiful decorations, *like* flowers made from sugar.
3 In Bermuda, *for instance*, the couple have two cakes.
4 In Korea, *for example* couples have long noodles called 'kuk soo'.

7 Look at each phrase in Exercise 6 and answer the questions.

1 Which two ways of introducing examples can be followed by a noun?
2 Which two ways of introducing examples can be followed by a subject and verb or by a comma and a noun?

8 Write examples in the gaps to complete the sentences.

1 I love eating sweet things such as *chocolate and puddings*.
2 At birthday parties in my country people eat food such as *feshbermen and pelay*.
3 In winter people usually prefer hot foods, for instance *kespe: soup*.
4 My favourite foods are things like *lagmen: noodles in sauce*
5 I don't like eating *sweet* foods, for example *cake and chocolate*.

9 Work in pairs. Think of festivals or celebrations in your country. Discuss the type of food that people usually eat at these festivals.

CRITICAL THINKING

At the end of this unit you are going to do the speaking task below.

> Discuss a new festival and make suggestions for events. Give a poster presentation about your festival to the rest of your group.

CREATE

1 Look at the photographs. Work with a partner. For each one answer the following questions.

   1 What is happening in each photograph?
   2 Have you ever been to this type of event or show?
   3 Where does this type of event or show usually happen?
   4 What do people do when they are there?
   5 Is there food and drink? What kind?

2 Write your answers to the questions in Exercise 1 in the table.

Type of festival	Ideas			
	Time and place	Food and drink	Activities	Sights and sounds
Sports event				
Motor show				

Organizing ideas

Use a four column table to organize ideas about a complicated topic. Only write one or two words in each section to quickly generate a lot of information about the topic before you start speaking.

SPEAKING

PREPARATION FOR SPEAKING

1 Put the words below in the correct order to make suggestion phrases.

1 this / could / You / online / look at /. _You could look at this online_

2 starting / How / wedding cake / ? / with / about _How about starting with wedding cake?_

3 not / Why / yourself / ? / try it _Why not try it yourself?_

2 Tick the phrases which make suggestions.

1 I will try that. ☐

2 Can I try? ☐

3 I'd suggest trying this. ☑

4 Shall we try this? ☑

5 Can we think about trying this? ☑

3 Write the suggestion phrases from Exercise 1 and Exercise 2 in the gaps to complete the table.

Infinitive without to	Verb -ing
1 _You could look at..._ .	4 _How about starting with_ ?
2 _Why not try it..._ ?	5 _I'd suggest trying this_ .
3 _Shall we try this_ ?	6 _Can we think about trying this_ ?

4 Write the suggestion phrases from Exercise 3 in the gaps to complete the dialogue. Try not to use the same expression more than once.

Woman: Isn't this great! There is so much to do!

Man: Yes. Fantastic. What do you want to do first?

Woman: (1) _Shall_ we go to the food tent? I'd like to get a drink.

Man: Ok. Good idea. After that (2) _how about_ visiting the art exhibition? I'd like to see some of the paintings.

Woman: Yes that sounds good. Then we (3) _could_ go and do a singing workshop.

Man: Oh I am not sure if that is a good idea. I am a terrible singer!

Woman: Ok, well (4) _how about_ listening to the talk on poetry instead?

Man: Yes I'd love to! That's a great idea!

Woman: What (5) _could_ we do after that?

Man: By then we will probably need to go home!

5 Work in pairs. Read the dialogue aloud with your partner. Did you choose similar phrases?

6 Look at the answers in the dialogue to each suggestion. Find one way to say 'no' and four ways to say 'yes' to the suggestions.

7 Read the website about the festival season in Singapore. Find two things you would like to do.

Mid-autumn Mooncake Festival

At this festival you can try some of the delicious moon cakes which taste of lotus, a type of flower that is found on top of water. You will see beautiful paper lanterns and you can watch some traditional dances.

Dragon Boat Race

If you are a sports fan you must see this race! Watch as teams from all over the world race their boats along the river then try it yourself in our practice boats!

The Singapore Arts Festival

Do you like the arts? Are you interested in music, theatre and performance? If you are don't miss this fantastic festival.

The Singapore Garden Festival

At this festival you can see wonderful gardens of all kinds. Some of them look like they are from films. There is an orchid garden and you can learn how to make a beautiful balcony garden too.

8 Work in a group of three. Discuss the events at the festival you would like to go to. Make suggestions to your group and use phrases from the dialogue in Exercise 4 on page 45 to say 'yes' or 'no' to their suggestions. Try to agree on two choices for your group.

UNL⊙CK LISTENING AND SPEAKING SKILLS 2

SPEAKING TASK

Discuss a new festival and make suggestions for events. Give a poster presentation about your festival to the rest of your group.

1 Work with a partner and think about the type of festival you would like to offer. Write some notes in the table.

Type of festival	Ideas			
	Time and place	Food and drink	Activities	Sights and sounds

2 Look at the following poster presentation for the Singapore Mosaic Music Festival. How many different sections can you see on the poster?

SINGAPORE MOSAIC MUSIC FESTIVAL

— When & where?

Location: the Esplanade, Theatre on the Bay.
March every year: get your tickets now!

— History of the festival

This 10 day festival began in 2007 and offers music for all ages. 60% of the music is free so everyone can come. Types of music include jazz, rap, blues and classical.

— Eating & cookery

Try the different dishes of Singapore: food from China, India, Malaysia, Thailand and more.
Learn to cook Asian speciality dishes from professional chefs.

— Sports

Try swimming at Sentosa Island on the beautiful beaches only 15 minutes away.

— Nature

Visit Bukit Timah Nature Reserve and see Singapore's biggest rain forest.

3 Work with a partner. Follow the instructions.

    1 Discuss how to present the information in the table on a poster.

    2 Think about how much writing you will include.

    3 Discuss how to make your poster look nice so that it helps to present your festival well.

4 Create your poster with a partner.

5 Complete the notes below to help you present your poster.

> Our festival is about _____ [*write the type of festival*].
> It takes place in _____ [*place*] in _____ [*month*].
> At the festival you can _____ [*activities*].
> You can eat _____ .
> You can drink _____ .
> You can see _____ .
> You can hear _____ .

6 Work in groups of four. Present your poster to the rest of the group giving examples of what you will offer. If you are listening, ask questions. In your groups, choose the best presentation and poster. Which festival would you like to go to?

TASK CHECKLIST	✔
Can you form questions using the Present simple and Present continuous?	
Have you learnt which vocabulary items often collocate?	
Can you make suggestions and say yes or no to them?	

OBJECTIVES REVIEW

I can ...

understand a film about a
New Year celebration.

very
well

not very
well

listen and take notes.

very
well

not very
well

analyze information.

very
well

not very
well

make suggestions.

very
well

not very
well

give a poster
presentation.

very
well

not very
well

WORDLIST

UNIT VOCABULARY	
activity (n)	have a celebration / a party (phr)
band (n)	have fun / a nice time / a problem
bride (n)	(phr)
camel (n)	interesting / interested in (adj)
celebration (n)	layer (n)
culture (n)	lecture (n)
decoration (n)	noodle (n)
dish (n)	take advice (phr)
dried fruit (n)	take an exam / a test (phr)
entertainment (n)	take care (phr)
festival (n)	take your time (phr)
groom (n)	traditional (adj)

LEARNING OBJECTIVES

Watch and listen	Watch and understand a video about schools in different countries
Listening skills	Use visual clues to listen; listen for detail
Speaking skills	Offer opinions, agree and disagree
Speaking task	Hold a debate whether students should choose how they learn

UNLOCK YOUR KNOWLEDGE

Work in pairs. Look at the photograph and answer the questions.

1 Have you ever learnt something in the way you can see in the photograph? Was it a good way to learn?

2 Talk about something you learnt outside the classroom. How did you learn? Did you enjoy it? Why?

3 Do you plan to learn something new? If yes, what would you like to learn?

4 What do you think will happen to schools and learning in the future?

WATCH AND LISTEN

PREPARING TO WATCH

1 You are going to watch a video about students in China, India and South Africa. Before you watch, choose the correct definition (a or b) for each word in bold (1–8). Use a dictionary to help you.

1 **primary school** This is a type of school for
   a older children e.g. between 11 and 18 years old.
   b younger children e.g. between 5 and 11 years old.

2 **high school** This is a type of school for
   a older children e.g. between 11 and 18 years old.
   b younger children e.g. between 5 and 11 years old.

3 **education** Getting an education means
   a having a job and earning money.
   b learning different subjects at school or university.

4 **training** This is learning
   a skills for a sporting activity e.g. football training.
   b a school subject e.g. Maths or History.

5 **martial arts** These are
   a art activities e.g. painting pictures.
   b traditional sports from China or Japan e.g. kung fu.

6 **feed** When you feed a child you
   a teach them.
   b give them food.

7 **pass** When we pass an exam
   a we do well.
   b we do badly.

8 **results** When we get the results of an exam we find out
   a if we passed or failed.
   b the time of the exam.

2 Write the correct form of the words in bold from Exercise 1 in the gaps to complete the sentences.

1 Getting good _results_ in an exam is important to most students.
2 If you have a good _education_ you will get a good job.
3 Children in _primary_ school usually have time to play games; they don't just study.
4 We should give money to _feed_ hungry or poor people in other countries.
5 When young people are at _high school_ they should start thinking about which job they want to do or which university they want to go to.
6 Students should have dictionaries and calculators in exams to help them to _pass_ .
7 If you want to be good at sports you should do some _training_ every day and you will get better.
8 Learning _martial arts_ can help you get fit and protect yourself.

3 Work in pairs. Discuss whether you agree or disagree with the sentences in Exercise 2.

4 Work in pairs. Discuss whether you think schools are the same or different from each other in China, India and South Africa.

WHILE WATCHING

5 ▶ Watch the video and check your ideas from Exercise 4.

6 Complete the sentences below with the numbers in the box.

LISTENING FOR KEY INFORMATION

106   300   37   1st   14   10

1 In China there are about _37_ students in each class in primary school.
2 In India, Anuj has exactly _106_ friends.
3 Thobela walks _10_ kilometres to school each day.
4 She is _14_ years old.
5 Thobela wants to be the _1st_ person in her family to go to high school and university.
6 Her school feeds _300_ children every day.

7 ▶ Watch again. Check your answers.

DISCUSSION

8 Work in pairs. Answer the questions.

1 Is it important to go to university in your country? Why?
2 What kind of jobs are popular? Do you need special education to do them?

PREPARING TO LISTEN

UNDERSTANDING
KEY VOCABULARY

1 You are going to listen to some visitors on a tour of a university. Write the words in the box next to the categories (1–3). Use the glossary on page 201 to help you.

> classroom Biology Physics teacher computer room
> laboratory French Chemistry Geography History lecturer
> library Art Maths corridor office stairs

1 subjects *Biology, Physics, French, Chemistry, Geography, History, Art, Maths,*

2 places *class room, computer room, laboratory, library, corridor, office, stairs*

3 people *teacher, lecturer*

PRONUNCIATION FOR LISTENING

2 Work in pairs. Say each word in Exercise 1 aloud, count the number of syllables and decide which syllable is stressed. Then complete the table.

Lecturer has three syllables and the first one is stressed.

A ●	B ●○	C ●○○	D ○●○○
_____	_____	lecturer	_____
_____	_____	_____	_____
_____	_____	_____	
_____	_____	_____	
		_____	
		_____	

3 Work in groups of three. Discuss which subjects at school you like / liked and which you are / were good at. Give reasons for your answer.

Using visual clues

When you listen, pictures and maps can help you to understand what you will hear. Look at maps and visual clues first and think about what you can see. Then when you listen you will already understand some of the content.

4 Look at the map of a university building below. Work in pairs and answer the questions.

USING VISUAL CLUES
TO LISTEN

1 Which rooms are labelled on the map?
2 What can you do there?
3 Describe the positions of room a, b, c, d, e and f.
Room c is on the left of room a.

WHILE LISTENING

5 🔊 **3.1** Listen to the tour of the university. Complete the map with places 1–7.

UNLØCK
ONLINE

1 ~~library~~   4 lecture theatre   7 computer room
2 canteen   5 events office
3 laboratories   6 international office

6 🔊 **3.1** Listen again and match the places 1–7 to the functions (a–g)

1 canteen *d*
2 library *e* ✓
3 laboratories *g* ✓
4 lecture theatre *b* ✓
5 events office *f* ✓
6 international office *a*
7 computer room *c*

a you can get advice
b you learn about History and Geography
c you need your university ID card
d you serve yourself
e you can make photocopies
f you can join clubs
g you can study Science

POST-LISTENING

7 Match the sentence beginnings (1–3) to the endings (a–c) to make sentences that express purpose (why we go to a place and what we can do there).

1 It's a really useful place to go *a*
2 It's a really useful place to go to *c*
3 It's a really useful place where *b*

a for help with visas.
b you can get help with visas.
c get help with visas.

8 Write sentences about the places in bold with the words in brackets. Use the example sentences in Exercise 7 to help you.

1 **a canteen** (food / to eat)
   a canteen is a place where you can eat a.
2 **a library** (books / to read)
   A library is a place where we can read a lot of food.
3 **a lecture theatre** (information / to learn)
   a l.t. is place where you can learn.

DISCUSSION

9 Work in pairs and answer the questions.

1 Which places in a school or university do you / did you use the most?
2 Do you remember your first school? Can you describe it?
3 Do you have a plan or purpose for your education or job? What is it?

⊙ LANGUAGE DEVELOPMENT

COLLOCATIONS ABOUT LEARNING

1 Look at the list of verbs in bold and subjects below from the listening. Decide which verb is different from the others. Use the glossary on page 201 to help you.

    1 **study**   Geography
    2 **learn**   Biology
    3 **teach**   French
    4 **revise**   History

2 Write verbs from Exercise 1 in the gaps to complete the sentences.

    1 You can _study_ a lot of subjects at school but most people only do one at university.
    2 It is not easy to _learn_ a new language. It takes a lot of time and effort to be able to speak or write it well.
    3 It's a good idea to _revise_ a lot before an exam.

3 Work in pairs. Discuss whether you think the sentences in Exercise 2 are true or false. Give reasons for your answers.

REVIEW OF PREPOSITIONAL PHRASES

4 Underline the prepositional phrases in the sentences from Listening 1.

    1 We are <u>in front of the stairs</u> <u>in the main hall</u>.
    2 The canteen where you can have lunch is <u>opposite the stairs</u>.
    3 <u>On the right</u>, <u>next to the canteen</u>, is the international office.
    4 Just <u>to the left of the canteen</u> is the events office.
    5 The first room <u>on the left</u> is the library.
    6 The second <u>on the left</u> is a computer room.
    7 The science laboratories are <u>on the first floor</u>.

5 Work in small groups. Discuss the difference in meaning between the pairs of sentences. Use the glossary on page 201 to help you.

    1 a You can find the computer room behind the library.
       b You can find the computer room opposite the library.
    2 a She lives near the university.
       b She lives next to the university.
    3 a The lecture is in the lecture theatre just to the right of the canteen.
       b The lecture is in the lecture theatre, it's the second room on the right, past the canteen.

UNLOCK ONLINE

BASIC VERB PATTERNS

6 Underline the main verbs in the sentences and look at the verb that follows.

1 Homework is important because I <u>want to pass</u> my exams.
2 Tim <u>enjoyed studying</u> French.
3 I <u>started to apply</u> to universities a month ago.
4 The lecturer <u>began talking</u> but had to stop to drink some water.
5 She didn't <u>mind helping</u> her friend with grammar exercises.
6 He <u>apologized for being</u> late for class.
7 They <u>are planning</u> on going abroad for a year to work.
8 My mum <u>began to learn</u> Arabic when she moved to Dubai.
9 I <u>started getting</u> headaches because I was watching TV for too long.
10 The lecturer <u>agreed to answer</u> more questions.

7 When two verbs come together, they usually follow one of the patterns below. Add the infinitive form of the verbs and the sentences from Exercise 6 to the table.

verb & preposition followed by verb + *ing*	verb followed by infinitive or verb + *ing*	verb followed by infinitive (*to* + verb)	verb followed by verb + *ing*
concentrate on The course concentrated on reading and writing	prefer Do you prefer to work alone or do you prefer working in a group?	decide She decided to take maths.	finish I finished doing my homework
1 apologize for	3 start	5 want to pass	7 enjoy
2 plan on	4 begin	6 agree to	8 mind

8 Write the correct form of the verb in brackets in the gaps to complete the sentences. Use the table above to help you.

1 I started _learning_ / _to learn_ (learn) languages because I'm very interested in travelling.
2 I switched off the TV to concentrate on _reading_ (read) the newspaper.
3 She wanted _to speak_ (speak) to the teacher at the end of the English lesson.
4 What are you planning on _doing_ (do) after class?
5 She began _to work_ / _working_ (work) at the office last year.
6 Would he agree _to help_ (help) if we pay him?
7 What time will your boss finish _talking_ (talk about) the project?
8 He has decided _to leave_ (leave) his job.
9 I apologized for _driving_ (drive) too fast.
10 I don't mind _playing_ (pay) to join a club because it's a great way to make new friends.
11 I enjoyed _discussing_ (discuss) Italian art even though I don't know much about it.

PREPARING TO LISTEN

1 Look at the photographs. What kind of technology are the students and teachers using to learn?

2 Work in pairs. You are going to listen to some trainee teachers talking about using technology to learn. Discuss whether you think technology helps learning.

UNL🔒CK
ONLINE

PRONUNCIATION FOR LISTENING

3 Look at the sentence below from Listening 2. Do you think the person is agreeing or disagreeing?

> Yes that's true.

Understanding intonation

It can be as important to listen to intonation as the words being spoken to know if a person agrees or disagrees.

4 🔊 **3.2** Listen to the sentence twice. Each time, decide if the person is agreeing (voice falls) or disagreeing (voice falls and then rises). Circle the correct word.

1 *agreeing / disagreeing*
2 *agreeing / disagreeing*

5 🔊 **3.3** Listen to more sentences from Listening 2. For each sentence, decide if the person is agreeing or disagreeing. Circle the correct word.

1 *agreeing / disagreeing*   3 *agreeing / disagreeing*
2 *agreeing / disagreeing*   4 agreeing / disagreeing

WHILE LISTENING

6 🔊 **3.4** Listen to the trainee teachers and number the ways of learning below in the order that you hear them discussed.

a using computers but just to do exercises _____

b doing an online course _____

c using a mobile device e.g. tablet or phone to learn _____

d blended learning (a mixture of online and classroom learning) _____

7 🔊 **3.4** Listen again. Match the person (1–3) to the opinion (a–e). More than one person may match an opinion.

1 Sarah	a Online learning really works.
2 Nazlihan	b Working in a traditional classroom is better.
3 Peter	c Having a teacher to talk to face to face helps.
	d Learning vocabulary on a smartphone is helpful.
	e Blended learning works well.

POST-LISTENING

8 Work in pairs. Divide the sentences below from the listening (1–5) into the two categories (a and b).

a agreement _____ _____ _____

b polite disagreement _____ _____

1 I probably agree with Sarah: I prefer having a teacher there to help me.

2 Yes, but on the other hand it isn't the same as speaking to someone.

3 Yes that's true Nazlihan! Mobile learning is great.

4 I agree that it is convenient but I don't like the small screen.

5 I think you are right.

DISCUSSION

9 Look at the following statements about learning. Decide if you agree or disagree and why.

1 We will always have teachers and classrooms.

2 Learning online can help people learn quickly.

3 Mobile learning is dangerous because students don't work, they send messages or chat.

10 Work in groups of three. Discuss each sentence in Exercise 9. Agree or politely disagree and give reasons.

CRITICAL THINKING

At the end of this unit you are going to do the speaking task below.

Hold a debate about whether students should choose how they learn. Explain if you agree or disagree with your classmates during the debate.

Holding a debate

A debate is a formal discussion of a topic. Before a debate each team needs to think about the topic and plan their argument. A *chairperson* controls the debate.

UNDERSTAND

1 The words in the box will be useful for your debate. Write the words in the correct section of the idea wheel.

> teacher   classroom   traditional   primary school   lecturer
> online   computer room   laboratory   blended   student

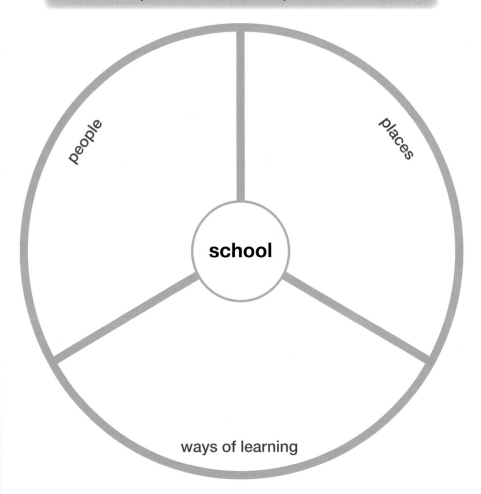

2 Look at the debating topic in the diagram below and decide if you are 'for' it (you agree with it) or 'against' it (you disagree with it).

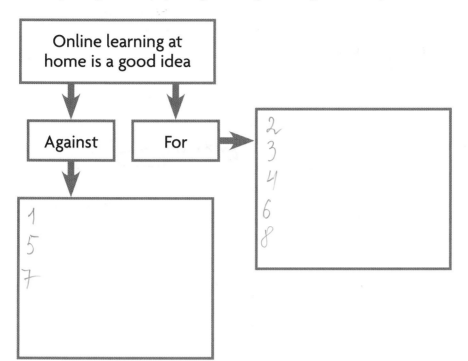

3 Work in pairs. Decide whether the sentences below are arguments 'for' or 'against' the debating topic in Exercise 2. Make notes in the diagram above.

1 You can't learn very well without someone helping you to understand.
2 Nowadays, you can find everything you need on the internet.
3 It is important for people to learn to study on their own with no teacher.
4 There aren't enough schools and classrooms for the high number of students. You don't need a school to learn online.
5 It's difficult to discuss ideas on the computer.
6 Some students live a long way from a school. It is difficult for them to get to school.
7 Going to school isn't just about learning a subject. It's also about learning social skills.
8 You can't study some subjects on the computer very easily e.g. Chemistry (you need a laboratory), Art (you need special equipment).

4 Work in pairs. Think of some more arguments for and against the debating topic. Add them to the diagram in Exercise 2.

5 Work in pairs. Take turns to read the debating topic from Exercise 2 out loud and to agree or disagree with your partner using sentences from Exercise 3 and your own ideas. Use *yes, but ...* or *yes I agree ...* and the correct intonation.

SPEAKING

PREPARATION FOR SPEAKING

1 Work in pairs. Answer the questions about the photographs.

   1 Which type of skill are the people in the photographs learning?

   2 Have you ever learnt any of these skills? If not, which one would you like to do and why?

   3 Why do you think people like learning these types of skill?

   4 Which other hobbies or interests can you think of that need you to learn a new skill?

2 Read the topic for a debate and underline the key words.

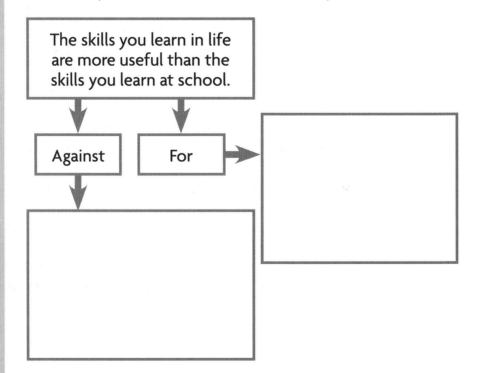

The skills you learn in life are more useful than the skills you learn at school.

Against

For

3 Think of three arguments for and against the debating topic. Add them to the flow chart in Exercise 2.

4 Work in pairs. Compare your ideas. Add your partner's ideas to your flow chart.

UNL🔓CK YOUR KNOWLEDGE

Work in pairs. Look at the photograph and answer the questions.

1 What kind of technology do you use every day at home, at school or at work?

2 Which kind of technology would be difficult to live without?

3 Can you think of examples of technology used in medicine, communication and entertainment?

4 Do you think there are disadvantages to technology? What are they?

PREPARING TO WATCH

1 Work in pairs. Match a word from the box with each definition 1–8.

> helmet   screen   diving   tank   submarine   shark
> virtual reality   projector

1 the sport of swimming under water
2 a hard hat to protect your head
3 a large or small pool or box used to keep fish
4 a flat surface where a film or picture is shown
5 electronic equipment which sends a picture from a computer onto a bigger surface
6 a large fish with sharp teeth and a fin on its back sometimes seen above water
7 images and sounds produced by a computer to make a new 'world' which seems real
8 a ship that can travel under water

2 Work in small groups and discuss whether you would like to do any of these things. Give reasons for your answers.

1 go diving in a sea where you can find sharks
2 ride a motorbike with no helmet
3 keep a fish tank with different fish at home
4 have a projector and a cinema screen at home to watch films
5 travel under water in a submarine
6 experience virtual reality

WHILE WATCHING

3 ▶ Watch the video and choose the correct answer.

1 At the beginning of the film you can see *four / five* divers.
2 The virtual reality space shows *the world / the moon*.

3 The scientists testing the virtual space are *making notes / laughing*.

4 The scientists look at the shark from *above the tank / under the tank*.

5 To film the sharks there are *some / no* divers in the tank with the mini submarine and camera.

6 The round screen put into the swimming pool is *white / glass*.

7 The swimming pool is made *light / dark*.

8 The diver in the swimming pool *can / can't* see film projected from the shark tank.

4 Write the correct words in the gaps to complete the sentences.

1 Diving is popular but not everyone can do it because sometimes it is
  e_____ and the best diving places are too
  f_____ a_____ .

2 When you go diving you usually wear a h_____ but
  scientists here are wearing special g_____ .

3 Many people would like to dive with sharks but usually they need
  special t_____ to do this.

4 Scientists use a mini-submarine to put a c_____ in the tank
  so they can film.

5 From the swimming pool the video of the s_____ can
  clearly be seen.

5 ▶ Watch the video again. Check your answers to Exercise 4.

DISCUSSION

6 Look at the advertisement. Work in small groups and discuss the questions.

1 Would you like to 'swim with sharks' in virtual reality? Why / why not?

2 Read the following advertisement for the 'Virtual Sea Adventure' and answer the questions:
  a Which two things can you do?
  b What can't you do?

7 In your groups, think of a virtual reality experience you would like to have. Create an advertisement.

8 Show your group's advertisement to the class. Listen to the ideas of the other groups. Then decide in your group which virtual reality experience you would like to have.

VIRTUAL SEA ADVENTURE
Swim with the sharks safely

Have the experience of a lifetime … come and swim with sharks in our special pool!

• you can see the sharks up close
• you can swim alongside them
• you can't get hurt!

PREPARING TO LISTEN

UNDERSTANDING
KEY VOCABULARY

1 You are going to listen to a student radio programme about robots. What can you see in each photograph?

2 Match the words in the box to the photographs in Exercise 1.

suit   water pollution   fish   disabled person   kitchen

PRONUNCIATION FOR LISTENING

3 Work in pairs. Say the words in Exercise 2 out loud and listen to the underlined sound. Then add each word to the sound maps below.

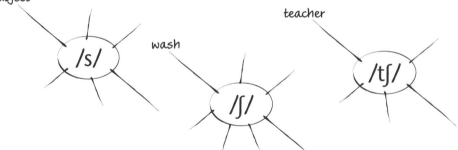

subject

/s/

wash

/ʃ/

teacher

/tʃ/

4 Add the words to the maps in Exercise 3.

1 na<u>ti</u>on
2 <u>s</u>ort
3 <u>sh</u>ort
4 wi<u>sh</u>
5 whi<u>ch</u>

6 math<u>s</u>
7 mat<u>ch</u>
8 o<u>c</u>ean
9 fa<u>c</u>e
10 <u>ch</u>eap

5 Read the sentences that have easily confused sounds and circle the correct word to complete the sentences.

1 Are there many *sorts / shorts* of robots?
2 Do you think robots are *sheep / cheap* or expensive?
3 Which things do you think robots do:
    a factory work?
    b household chores for old people e.g. <u>watching</u> clothes?
    c cookery?
    d medical care?
    e measuring pollution in the *sea / she* ?
    f police checks?
    g answering phones?

6 Work in pairs. Predict the answers to the questions in Exercise 5.

WHILE LISTENING

7 🔊 **4.1** Listen to the radio programme and check your predictions to your ideas in Exercise 5.

LISTENING FOR
MAIN IDEAS

Listening for reasons

People often talk about reasons for things happening. For example: I passed my exam because I worked hard. Working hard is the reason I passed my exam. When people give reasons for things, they use words like *as*, *because of* and *due to*. If you hear these you know a reason will follow.

8 🔊 **4.1** Listen again. Write the missing information in the gaps to complete the table.

UNL**O**CK
ONLINE

Event	Reason
Robots not used so much in the past	...as robots were 1 _____ .
People have a much better quality of life	...thanks to these 2 _____ .
Some old people can't do housework	...because of their 3 _____ .
We can find out about pollution quickly	...due to the 4 _____ .

POST-LISTENING

9 Use the words in the box to complete the sentences.

> as   Because of   due to   Thanks to

1 _____ wifi, she was able to do her work on her tablet in the café.
2 He couldn't use his laptop _____ a problem with the hard drive.
3 His laptop broke _____ he was careless and dropped it.
4 _____ a bad internet connection, he wasn't able to email me.

DISCUSSION

10 Work with a partner and answer the questions.

1 What ways have robots changed society?
2 Compare your ideas with another pair. Are they similar?
3 Are robots a good or bad thing? Give reasons for your answer.

⊙ LANGUAGE DEVELOPMENT

CAN / BE ABLE TO

1 Look at the sentences (1–9) from Listening 1 and answer the questions (a–c).

> 1 Robots **can** now assist people who can't walk.
> 2 Before the accident, Joey **could** surf very well.
> 3 He **wasn't** even **able to** sit up on his own when a visitor came.
> 4 He **couldn't** even feel his legs when doctors touched them.
> 5 But when he put on the robotic suit he **was able to** stand up and walk on his own again.
> 6 After the accident, Joey **couldn't** walk at all.
> 7 He **isn't able to** walk at all without the suit.
> 8 Old people, for example, **can't** always do housework easily.
> 9 The robot means they **are able to** stay in their own homes.

a Which sentences are about now? Which are about the past?
b Which sentences are negatives? How do you create the negative form for *can / could* and *be able to*?
c Which verb isn't followed by *to*?

EXPLANATION

2 Write verb forms from Exercise 1 in the gaps to complete the rules in the box.

> (1)_____ (+) / (2)_____ (-) and (3)_____ (+) / (4)_____ (-) are used to talk about general ability in the present.
>
> (5)_____ (+) / (6)_____ (-) are used to talk about general ability in the past.
>
> (7)_____ (+) / (8)_____ (-) and (9)_____ (-) are used to talk about ability in particular situations in the past.

3 Circle the correct verb form to complete the sentences.

1 *I can / am able* to swim quite well but I don't like going under the water.

2 Mohammed *could / was able to* speak when he was two years old but his brother didn't learn until much later.

3 Sunita *could / was able to* speak a little when the doctor asked her how she was after an operation on her mouth.

4 My little sister *couldn't / wasn't able to* hear very well when she was young.

5 Jade *wasn't able to / couldn't* open the car door so she climbed out of the window.

4 Write down an activity in each box below.

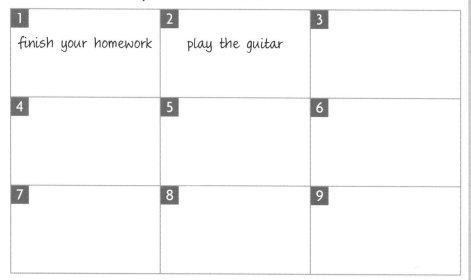

1 finish your homework	2 play the guitar	3
4	5	6
7	8	9

5 Work in pairs. Take turns to choose a number from the grid above. Your partner should ask you if you *can / are able to* do the activity in the box with that number. Give reasons for your answer.

TECHNOLOGY

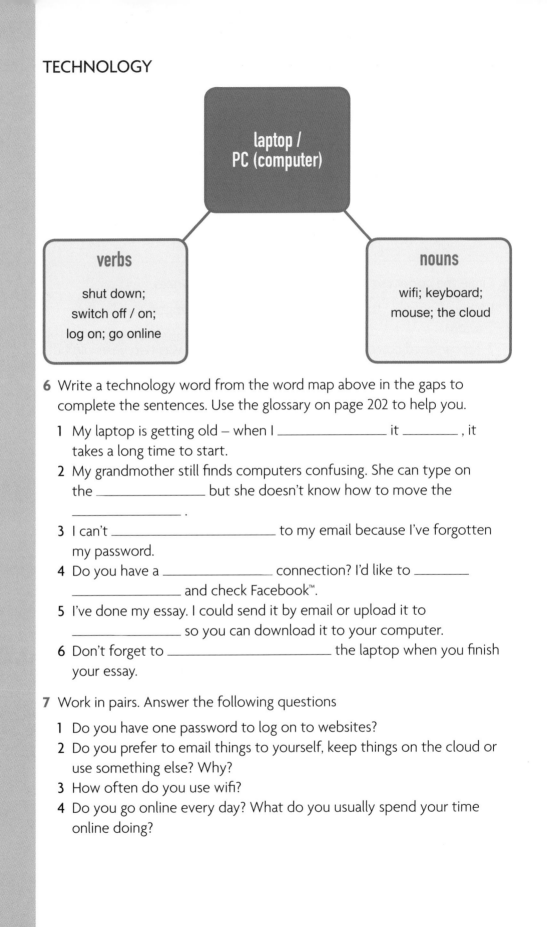

laptop / PC (computer)

verbs

shut down;
switch off / on;
log on; go online

nouns

wifi; keyboard;
mouse; the cloud

6 Write a technology word from the word map above in the gaps to complete the sentences. Use the glossary on page 202 to help you.

1 My laptop is getting old – when I _____ it _____ , it takes a long time to start.

2 My grandmother still finds computers confusing. She can type on the _____ but she doesn't know how to move the _____ .

3 I can't _____ to my email because I've forgotten my password.

4 Do you have a _____ connection? I'd like to _____ _____ and check Facebook™.

5 I've done my essay. I could send it by email or upload it to _____ so you can download it to your computer.

6 Don't forget to _____ the laptop when you finish your essay.

7 Work in pairs. Answer the following questions

1 Do you have one password to log on to websites?

2 Do you prefer to email things to yourself, keep things on the cloud or use something else? Why?

3 How often do you use wifi?

4 Do you go online every day? What do you usually spend your time online doing?

8 Put the words in the box below into the correct place on the word map. One of the words is both a verb and a noun.

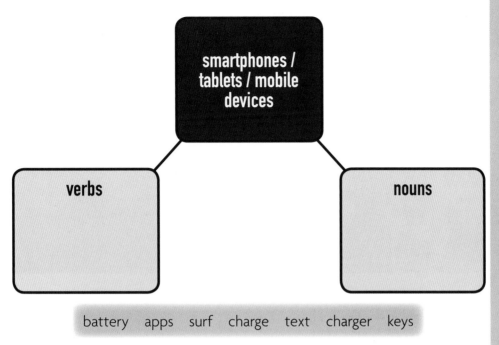

battery   apps   surf   charge   text   charger   keys

9 Write the words from the map in Exercise 9 in the gaps to complete the sentences.

1 Do you have a touchscreen phone or one with _____ that you press?

2 If you have a tablet or smartphone, which are your favourite _____ and websites? Why?

3 How often do you _____ the net to find information? What kind of things do you look for?

4 Do you prefer to phone and speak to people or _____ them? Why?

5 Has your phone's _____ ever run out of power and stopped working at a bad time? What happened?

6 Do you take your _____ with you so you can _____ your phone at any time?

10 Work in pairs. Ask and answer the questions.

PREPARING TO LISTEN

UNDERSTANDING
KEY VOCABULARY

1 You are going to listen to a news report about how computers affect our memory. Match the words (1–7) to their definitions (a–g). Then check your answers in the glossary on page 202.

1	stupid	a	to study something in detail to understand it a lot
2	memory	b	not clever or intelligent
3	research	c	the opposite of 'easy'
4	difficult	d	where information is stored or saved on a computer
5	scientist	e	the place where something is found
6	location	f	the ability to remember information, experiences and people
7	computer file	g	a person who works in or studies science

PRONUNCIATION FOR LISTENING

2 The news reporter uses linking words to add supporting examples or details to the key information. Underline the linking words in the sentences below.

1 You will hear main information and additional information.
2 You will hear main information as well as additional information.

3 Think about the sounds in the linking words.

1 Which letter do we often not say when we use *and*?
2 Is the letter *a* in *and* strong /æ/ or weak /ə/?
3 Is the letter *a* in the phrase *as well as* strong /æ/ or weak /ə/?

4 Work in pairs. Say the sentences in Exercise 2 aloud and pronounce the sounds correctly.

WHILE LISTENING

5 🔊 **4.2** Listen to the report and write the missing information in the gaps to complete the main information in the first column of the table.

**UNL⌀CK
ONLINE**

main information	additional details
Scientists looked, in particular, at how computers affect our (1)____memory____	They wanted to find out if computers have changed the way we remember (6)_____ and knowledge.
What we think when we are asked (2)_____ questions has changed due to (3)_____ like Google™.	In the past people tried to think of the (7)_____ to the question. Now people think about (8)_____ to find the answer. e.g. They think about what they might (9)_____ into Google™.
The type of (4)_____ we remember has changed.	People now forget (10)_____ especially if they know it will be saved on the computer. They remember the (11)_____ of the fact, in other words, where to find it.
Computers are not making us more stupid but they are making us (5)_____ .	We are spending time remembering where to (12)_____ information but not on remembering the information itself.

6 🔊 **4.2** Listen again and complete the additional details in the second column of the table.

DISCUSSION

7 Write down one type of information you keep:
a on your computer b on your smartphone c in the 'cloud'.

8 Work in pairs. Compare your answers to Exercise 7.

I keep my photos in the 'images' file on my phone and my essays in the 'studies' file on my laptop.

9 Work in pairs. Discuss possible problems with keeping information on your computer or in the cloud.

CRITICAL THINKING

At the end of this unit you are going to do the speaking task below.

> Present a report about technology, providing some information about a device. Look at advantages and disadvantages and give details to support the main ideas.

REMEMBER

1 Work in pairs. Discuss the questions.

　1 How many mobile devices do you have and what do you use them for?
　2 What do you download most and why?
　3 Do you use social networks?

2 Look at the three sentences about social networks. Decide if they are advantages (+) or disadvantages (−) and add them into the correct column in the table below.

　1 You can contact your friends online
　2 You can see your friends' latest news and photos
　3 You don't leave your home
　4 You can contact people who live far away
　5 You never speak to anyone anymore

main argument: Social networks have changed the way we communicate	
advantages (+)	disadvantages (−)

3 Work in pairs. Compare your ideas. Can you add any more advantages or disadvantages to the table?

4 Work in pairs. Choose one of the technologies below, write a main argument at the top of the table on page 81. Add some advantages (+) and disadvantages (−) in the columns.

> the internet　mobile phones　internet TV
> 3D TV　cars that work without a driver
> robot surgeons

main argument:	
advantages (+)	disadvantages (–)

5 Work in a different pair. Listen to their ideas. Do you have the same or different ideas?

SPEAKING

PREPARATION FOR SPEAKING

1 Write the words from the box in the gaps to complete the sentences. Sometimes more than one answer is possible. Use the glossary on page 202 to help you.

but   however   whereas   on the other hand

1 When people were asked difficult questions in the past scientists believe they tried to think of the answer to the question. _____ , because of modern websites the first thing people think about now is how to find the answer.

2 For example they think about what they might put into Google™, _____ in the past they thought about the question itself.

3 It seems that people now forget facts especially if they know the information will be saved in a computer file. _____ , an advantage is they remember the location of the fact and where to find it.

4 In conclusion, it seems that computers are not making us stupid, _____ they are making us lazy!

2 🔊 **4.3** Listen and check.

3 Circle the correct option to complete the rules about the words in bold.

But, **however**, **whereas**, and **on the other hand** link *similar ideas / link different information*.

4 Read sentences a–e. Do the words in bold introduce different information or additional information?

a People use computers to save information **and** to organize it.
b People use computers to save information **and also** to organize it.
c **Also** people use computers to save information and to organize it.
d People use computers to save information **as well as** organizing it.
e People use computers to save information and to organize it **too**.

5 Match the linking words in italics in the sentences (1–3) to the correct sentence ending (a or b) .

1 Computers help people look for things *and / but*
  a they can find information quickly.
  b they can make people lazy.
2 Technology is now important for our social lives *and also / , whereas*
  a traditional activities like writing letters are disappearing.
  b makes it easier for us to communicate with friends.
3 Robots assist people with difficult jobs *as well as / . However,*
  a helping with the care of old and disabled people.
  b some people believe they are bad because people lose their jobs when robots are used.

6 You are going to give a short report about technology to your partner.

1 Look at the advantages and disadvantages you wrote about technology in the Critical Thinking section, Exercise 4.
2 Make sentences about the main argument using language to give reasons from Listening 1, page 74.
3 Link additional information and different information using language from Preparation for speaking Exercises 1–4.

Social networks are important *because* they have changed the way we communicate. I don't speak to my friends on the phone *but* I can contact my friends online. I can contact people who live far away *as well* seeing their latest news and photos. *However,* I don't go out with my friends or leave my bedroom very much.

7 Read sentences a and b. Circle the correct option about the words in bold.

We use these expressions to *introduce / finish* what we are saying in a report.

a **To conclude**, social networks are a useful way to keep in contact with your friends, but you have to remember to speak to them and leave home sometimes!

b **In conclusion**, social networks are a useful way to keep in contact with your friends, but you have to remember to speak to them and leave home sometimes!

8 Add a sentence to your ideas in Exercise 6 to finish what you think about the technology you chose to talk about.

9 Work in pairs. Read your sentences about technology to your partner. Do you agree or disagree with your partner's ideas about technology?

SPEAKING TASK

Present a report about technology, providing some information about a device. Look at advantages and disadvantages and give details to support the main ideas.

1 Choose a different piece of technology from the list or use your own idea.

PREPARE

the internet   mobile phones   internet TV
3D TV   cars that work without a driver
robot surgeons

2 Follow the steps from the Preparation for speaking section, Exercises 6–8.

1 Use the table below to list your advantages and disadvantages.

main argument:	
advantages (+)	disadvantages (–)

2 Use the ideas from the table to write sentences with linking words.

3 Add a conclusion.

4 Complete these sentences with your ideas to start your report.

Today I am going to present my report on
_____ . [write the name of
the technology] The main argument I am going to present is
_____ [write the main
argument from your table].

PRACTICE

5 Practise the introduction to your report, the sentences to link advantages and disadvantages and the conclusion.

PRESENT

6 Present your report to your partner.

TASK CHECKLIST	✔
Have you used *can* and *be able to* correctly?	
Can you offer main information and supporting details using the correct language?	
Can you describe technology and technological devices?	
Have you linked sentences using words to contrast ideas or add extra information?	

OBJECTIVES REVIEW

I can ...

watch and understand a video about the virtual reality.

very well — not very well

hear and pronounce /s/ /ʃ/ /tʃ/.

very well — not very well

listen for reasons.

very well — not very well

analyse information for main ideas and supporting details.

very well — not very well

describe additional and contrasting information.

very well — not very well

present a report.

very well — not very well

WORDLIST

UNIT VOCABULARY		
advertise (v)	due to (prep)	shut down (v)
also (adv)	file (computer file) (n)	stupid (adj)
app (n)	go online (v)	suit (n)
as (adv)	however (adv)	surf (v)
as well as (adv)	keyboard (n)	switch on / off (v)
battery (n)	location (n)	text (n) (v)
because of (prep)	log on (prep)	thanks to (phr)
but (conj)	memory (n)	the cloud (n)
charger (n)	mouse (n)	water pollution (n)
difficult (adj)	on the other hand (phr)	whereas (adv)
disabled (adj)	research (n)	wifi (n)
download (v)	scientist (n)	

LEARNING OBJECTIVES

Watch and listen	Watch and understand a video about languages in South America
Listening skills	Listen for genre; listen for instructions
Speaking skills	Sequence instructions
Speaking task	Plan and give a set of instructions

LANGUAGE AND COMMUNICATION

UNLOCK YOUR KNOWLEDGE

Work in pairs. Look at the photograph and answer the questions.

1 When we communicate we share information with other people. How do people communicate with each other?

2 What can make communication difficult?

3 Do you think it is important to learn another language? Why / why not?

LISTENING 1

PREPARING TO LISTEN

USING YOUR
KNOWLEDGE TO
PREDICT CONTENT

1 Work in pairs. You are going to hear some information about four
different languages. Answer the questions.

   1 Do you know where India, the USA, Wales and Russia are? Which other
   countries are they close to?

   2 Which language is officially spoken in each country?

2 Look at the things we can use to help us understand when we listen.
Write *S* (things people say) or *O* (other clues).

   1 background music   _____

   2 a happy or enthusiastic voice   _____

   3 formal or informal words   _____

   4 background noises e.g. voices / traffic   _____

PRONUNCIATION FOR LISTENING

3 🔊 **5.1** Listen to the phrases. Write *P* (if the person sounds positive) or
S (if the person sounds serious).

   1 You should learn English! _____

   2 Come and learn with us! _____

   3 Don't forget to study! _____

4 Which phrase might be in an advertisement? How do you know?

5 🔊 **5.2** When we want something to sound positive, our voices often go
up at the end of the phrase. Listen and repeat the sentences.

   1 Come and learn with us!

   2 You should learn English!

   3 We can help!

   4 Come to us for lessons!

WHILE LISTENING

Listening for genre

When you listen for information, it can help if you know the type or 'genre' of the text. Genre describes the special characteristics of a text, e.g. a news report usually has one person speaking, it is factual and formal and it begins with a short description of the main stories. If you know the genre of a text you can make predictions, e.g. guess how many people will speak, the order of information and the words you may hear. This will help you understand quickly.

6 Work in pairs. Match the genre of listening in column A to the characteristics (a–h) in column B. There are two characteristics for each genre.

UNLOCK ONLINE

A genre	B characteristics
radio advertisement _e_ _____	**a** one speaker giving facts about recent events (not opinions) **b** one speaker describing objects and what we can learn from them
telephone message _____ _____	**c** the history of different objects **d** present tenses used to describe recent events
museum tour _____ _____	~~**e** fun music~~ **f** 'beep' sound
TV news report _____ _____	**g** someone giving their name / phone number **h** short sentences with positive adjectives

7 🔊 **5.3** Listen to the four recordings. Number the genre from Column A of the table in the order that you hear them.

radio advertisement   _____
telephone message   _____
museum tour   _____
TV news report   _____

8 Look at the photograph of Boa Senior. Do you remember which country she was from and which language she spoke?

9 🔊 5.3 Listen again. Write the country and the language that is in danger in the box in columns B and C to complete the table.

> Russia   Welsh   India   Bo   Wales   Tuva
> Navajo   America

A genre	B country	C language
1 television news report		
2 telephone message		
3 museum tour		
4 radio advertisement		

DISCUSSION

10 Work alone and write your answers to the questions.

1 Which language is the most important for people to learn?
2 Why should we try to keep languages which are in danger alive?

11 Talk to other students. Find two people who have similar ideas for each question.

⊙ LANGUAGE DEVELOPMENT

IMPERATIVE CLAUSES

1 Match the sentences from Listening 1 (a–d) to the rules in the grammar box (1–3). There are two examples for one of the rules.

UNLOCK
ONLINE

> **a** Visit our website and download the factsheet on endangered languages.
> **b** Please leave your name, number and a message after the beep.
> **c** Follow me, if you wouldn't mind.
> **d** … don't delay, get in touch today.

EXPLANATION

1 We use imperative clauses when we want to tell someone to do something. The clauses do not usually have a subject.

Open your books. Wait for me.

2 We also use imperative clauses when we want to tell someone not to do something. Negative imperatives use the auxiliary *do* + *not* + the infinitive without *to*. *Do not* is formal so in speaking negative imperatives use *don't*. We can use *don't* on its own in short answers.

A: Shall I call a taxi?
B: No don't. We can walk. It's not far.

3 Imperatives are a very direct way of speaking. To sound more polite, use *please* or, in formal situations, *if you wouldn't mind*.

Open your books please. Please wait for me
Please stay here if you wouldn't mind.

2 Correct the mistakes in these sentences.

1 You open your books.
2 Don't to be late.
3 Open it the window.
4 Come you back later.
5 Unlocking your screen please.

3 Rewrite these imperatives to make them more polite.

1 Listen to me. _____
2 Repeat your instructions. _____
3 Go back. _____
4 Speak more loudly. _____
5 Start again. _____

VERB PATTERNS

1 *Say* is indirect. We *say something* (*to someone*).

2 *Tell* is direct. We *tell someone something*. We can't *tell to someone something.*

3 We can *say something.*

4 We can use *that* after *say* but not directly after *tell.*

5 *Speak* is used with *to someone about something.*

6 *Ask* is used with *someone about something* or with *someone to do something.*

4 Look at the rules in the box above. Cross out the sentence in each pair (a and b) below which is incorrect.

1 **a** He said Tuvan is a type of Russian.
   b ~~He told Tuvan is a type of Russian.~~
2 **a** He said that Tuvan is a type of Russian.
   b He told that Tuvan is a type of Russian.
3 **a** He said Tuvan is a type of Russian.
   b He told to us Tuvan is a type of Russian.
4 **a** He said us Tuvan is a type of Russian.
   b He told us Tuvan is a type of Russian.
5 **a** We spoke someone.
   b We asked someone.
6 **a** We spoke to him about the end of Bo.
   b We asked to him about the end of Bo.
7 **a** We spoke him about the end of Bo.
   b We asked him about the end of Bo.

5 Find one word which does not form a collocation with the verb (*say* and *tell*).

1 We *tell the truth / a lie / the time / a story / the answer / someone about something.*
2 We *say hello and goodbye / something / the answer / me something.*

6 Write the correct form of *say, tell, speak* or *ask* to complete the sentences.

1 Could you _____ me the answer please?
2 Did you _____ to your new boss yesterday?
3 I always _____ the truth.
4 _____ me about the lecture.
5 I _____ Kate to tell me about her new job.

LISTENING 2

PREPARING TO LISTEN

1 Work in pairs. You are going to listen to someone who uses sign language to communicate. Discuss what sign language is and who uses it.

UNDERSTANDING
KEY VOCABULARY

2 Circle the word that is different from the others.

　1 *deaf / blind / tall*
　2 *pick up / find / learn*
　3 *head / palm / thumb*
　4 *chin / lip / smell*
　5 *wave / speak / pat*

3 Complete each sentence with the correct word from Exercise 2.

　1 He uses a white stick when he walks because he is _____ and it helps him find his way without falling.
　2 She is good at languages. She can _____ new words very quickly.
　3 He had some money in the _____ of his hand.
　4 He doesn't have a beard but he has a bit of hair on his _____ .
　5 You can _____ the horse if you like, but move slowly or you will scare it.

LISTENING FOR
MAIN IDEAS

4 🔊 **5.4** Listen and tick the correct option in each case.

1 Lana can
  a speak but she can't hear. ☐
  b understand but she can't speak. ☐
2 Lana is from
  a America. ☐
  b Jordan. ☐
3 Home language is a type of sign language
  a found in each country. ☐
  b found in a family. ☐
4 Most children born deaf will
  a pick up sign language at home. ☐
  b have lessons in sign language. ☐
5 Lana demonstrates the sign for
  a happy. ☐
  b tired. ☐

LISTENING FOR
INSTRUCTIONS

5 🔊 **5.5** Listen to an extract of the listening. Number the pictures in the correct order.

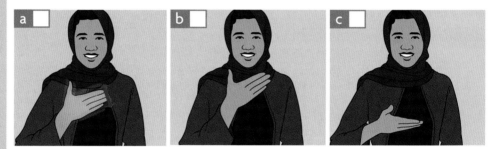

a ☐   b ☐   c ☐

POST-LISTENING

6 Work in pairs. Look at the pictures above and try to make the sign that is described.

7 Work with another pair. Compare your signs.

8 Work in pairs. Take turns to describe the sign we make with our hands when we want to communicate the messages (1–5) to another person.

  1 Hello! We hold our hand up with our palms facing towards the person and we wave.
  2 OK
  3 It smells bad!
  4 It's expensive.
  5 Please be quiet.

9 Work in pairs. Think of two more messages and signs.

PRONUNCIATION FOR LISTENING

10 Work in pairs. Say the words out loud.

 1 tell   2 told   3 talk   4 late

11 Each word has the letter *t*. Which other letter is in all the words? Does it sound the same each time?

12 Look at the word map. Find a route across the map from column 1 to 5 by finding words with a silent *l*. You can go across or down. You can't move diagonally.

	1	2	3	4	5
a	walk	let	leave	late	call
b	could	calm	please	listen	look
c	left	would	half	palm	letter
d	sell	light	blue	should	talk
e	sleep	flower	hello	lost	told

13 Work in pairs. Take turns to choose a word and tell your partner which column and row the word is in. Your partner will say the word aloud.

A: C4
B: palm

CRITICAL THINKING

At the end of this unit you are going to do the speaking task below.

> Plan and give a set of instructions.

REMEMBER

1 Think about Lana's description of the sign for happy from Listening 2 on page 96. Write the missing words into the gaps to create clear instructions.

   1 P_____ your hand in front of your chest with your palm up.

   2 P_____ your little finger near your chest.

   3 Make sure your th_____ is away from you.

   4 Move your hand up towards your c_____ in a quick movement.

   5 It should look like you are going to pat yourself u_____ the chin.

   6 Do it a few times quickly. This means you are h_____ !

Giving instructions

To give instructions, use a simple flow chart to help you think of the actions you will need to describe the process.

2 Work in pairs. Discuss the questions.

   1 What do you think this is a photograph of?

   2 What can you use the clock function to do?

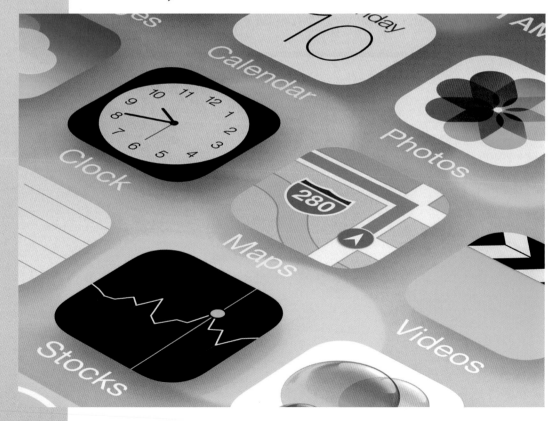

3 Complete the instructions for setting the alarm on a mobile phone. Write the verbs in the box in the flow chart.

put   enter   save   pick   unlock   select   press

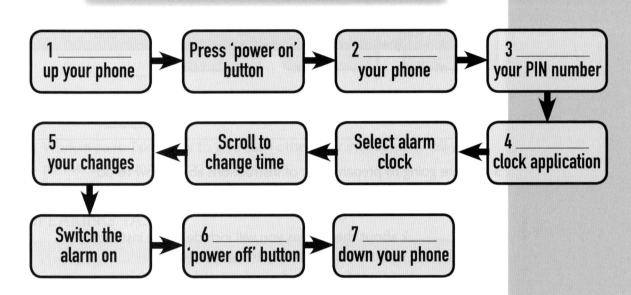

| 1 _____ up your phone | → | Press 'power on' button | → | 2 _____ your phone | → | 3 _____ your PIN number |

| 5 _____ your changes | ← | Scroll to change time | ← | Select alarm clock | ← | 4 _____ clock application |

| Switch the alarm on | → | 6 _____ 'power off' button | → | 7 _____ down your phone |

4 Change the instructions to make the flow chart work better for your phone.

5 Work with a partner. Give the instructions in the flowchart to your partner. Can your partner follow your instructions?

6 Work in pairs. Discuss the best way of communicating instructions for doing something new. Choose the best way for you from the list.

1 Another person shows you.
2 A list of written instructions is given to you.
3 You watch a podcast or a YouTube™ video showing you what to do.
4 You can ask questions on a website.

SPEAKING

PREPARATION FOR SPEAKING

1 🔊 5.5 In Listening 2, Lana uses sequencing words to show when each thing happens. Listen and number the words in the order that she uses them.

UNLOCK ONLINE

_____ first of all
_____ then
_____ next

LEARNING OBJECTIVES

Watch and listen	Watch and understand a video about rain
Listening skills	Predict ideas from research; recognize mood
Speaking skills	Explain consequences
Speaking task	Present the results of a survey about land use and the climate

UNLOCK YOUR KNOWLEDGE

Work in pairs. Look at the photograph and answer the questions.

1 What kind of weather do you prefer when you are working, studying or on holiday? Why?

2 Do you think the climate is changing in the world generally? Why?

3 Have you ever experienced water shortages or floods? Do you do anything in your daily life to try and help with these problems?

WATCH AND LISTEN

PREPARING TO WATCH

1 Match the words (1–5) to the correct definition (a–e).

1 heat   **a** to go up or get higher
2 rise   **b** powder of dirt or soil
3 dust   **c** the temperature of something or to make cold
4 droplet   **d** the temperature of something or to make hot or warm
5 cool   **e** a very small round amount of liquid e.g. water on
                   a window

2 Write *T* (true) or *F* (false) for each of the facts.

1 When we heat water, it boils when it reaches 100°C.   ____
2 When oil and water are mixed, the water rises to the top.   ____
3 20% of dust can be caused by vehicles travelling along roads.   ____
4 Water droplets form when gas changes back into liquid.   ____
5 If water cools enough it becomes ice.   ____

3 Work in pairs. Look at a photograph of the water cycle. Describe what happens using the words from Exercise 1.

WHILE WATCHING

4 ▶ Watch the video for the first minute without sound. Using your ideas from Exercise 3 guess what the presenter is saying.

5 ▶ Watch again with sound. Were your ideas correct?

6 Match the numbers (1–4) to the facts (a–d).

1	300 million	a	the percentage of extra rain people can make
2	5, 486	b	the time it takes to make the rain fall
3	45	c	the numbers of litres of rain that falls each day in the world
4	12	d	the height in metres that the aeroplane flies

7 ▶ Watch the rest of the video. Check your answers.

8 Read the questions below. Can you remember the answers?

1 What heats water and turns it into gas?
2 When the water cools it falls down again as rain, ice and in one other form. Can you name the third form?
3 What is the problem in Texas in the USA?
4 Where does Gary put silver iodide?
5 Why did Gary fly his plane into the clouds?

9 ▶ Watch the video again. Check your answers.

POST-LISTENING

10 Match the types of weather (1–7) with the climate words (a–g) which have a similar meaning. Use a dictionary to help you.

1	heavy rain	a	high temperatures
2	bright sunshine	b	gale-force winds
3	thick snow	c	extreme weather
4	strong winds	d	freezing conditions
5	thick fog	e	high rainfall
6	changing weather	f	foggy weather
7	very hot or cold weather	g	climate change

DISCUSSION

11 Work in pairs. Discuss the following questions.

1 What is the weather forecast for today and tomorrow?
2 Which country would you like to live in or visit because of the climate?
3 What do people in your country generally think about the idea of climate change? Do you agree or disagree? Why?
4 Can you think of examples of extreme weather?

LISTENING 1

PRONUNCIATION FOR LISTENING

1 Say the words in the groups (A and B) out loud. Which sound can you hear in all of the words in each group? (/ɒ/ /əʊ/)

A frog   forest   cost   want
B global   don't   known   won't

2 Work in pairs. Write a word from Exercise 1 in the gaps to complete the sentences.

1 We _____ have a rainy season in my country. It's much too dry.
2 Most people in my country _____ to stop climate change but they don't know how.
3 I often go walking in the _____ near where I live.
4 People have _____ about climate change for a long time but they haven't done much about it.
5 If we want to stop climate change, it will _____ a lot of money.

3 Work in pairs. Decide if sentences 1–3 in Exercise 2 are true or false for you. Say the sentences aloud before you discuss them.

PREPARING TO LISTEN

UNDERSTANDING
KEY VOCABULARY

1 You are going to listen to a news report. Before you do, look at the photograph. Which animal do you think it shows? Have you ever seen one before?

2 Read some information about The Western Ghats rainforest below. Summarize the information into three key points.

> The Western Ghats is a tropical rainforest located in the west of India. The rainforest has a short dry period each year but typically gets a lot of rain during the rainy season. However the type of weather in the forest is changing quickly and ^(a) <u>global warming</u> means that nowadays less rain falls. This is changing the forest itself, ^(b) <u>damaging</u> the environment and stopping growth. The rainforest is home to ^(c) <u>wildlife</u> of many different kinds and new ^(d) <u>species</u> are still being found. However the damage to the rainforests mean that some wildlife is ^(e) <u>disappearing,</u> killed by the changes in climate.

3 Compare your key points with a partner. Did you choose the same points?

4 In the listening you will hear the underlined words from the text in Exercise 2. Match the underlined words (a–e) to the definitions (1–5). Use the glossary on page 203 to help you.

 1 animals, birds and plants living in the natural environment
 2 air around the world becoming warmer because of pollution
 3 to stop existing in the world
 4 harming or causing a problem for a person or thing
 5 groups of plants or animals with similar characteristics

WHILE LISTENING

UNLOCK ONLINE

Predicting ideas from research

Before we listen to lectures, reports or information about a topic, we often have time to prepare. It helps to read some information in advance because you can learn about the key topic information and issues that people think are important. You can then predict the main ideas that you will hear.

5 Read the paragraph in Exercise 2 again. Tick the things on the list below that you think you will hear when you listen to the report.

 1 city names ☐
 2 information about the weather in the rainforest ☐
 3 facts about wildlife ☐
 4 the typical day of a scientist ☐
 5 information about effects of climate change ☐

PREDICTING IDEAS
FROM RESEARCH

6 🔊 **6.1** Listen and check.

6 Write *will*, *going to* or *the Present continuous* in the gaps to complete the rules in the box. Use Exercise 5 to help you.

Decisions and plans

1 We use _____ to talk about decisions made at the time you are speaking.

2 We use _____ to talk or ask about decisions made before you speak / a general plan which can change in the future.

3 We use _____ to talk about fixed arrangements made for the future. It is difficult to change these arrangements.

Predictions

4 We use *going to* when we have evidence to show the future event.

5 We use *will* when we are guessing or are not certain. We often use it with *probably*.

7 Write the correct future form of the verb in brackets in the gaps to complete the sentences. Sometimes there is more than one answer.

Decisions and plans

1 I've just finished packing. I _____ (leave) tonight at six o'clock to catch the train.

2 I haven't finished my project about global warming because I haven't got enough information. I've decided that I _____ (do) some more research on the internet.

3 'I _____ (go) to the garden centre this weekend. Does anyone want to come?' 'Ok, I _____' (come).

4 Professor Lang _____ (talk) about climate change in his lecture tomorrow.

Predictions

1 You are carrying too many books! You _____ (drop) them.

2 The exam was difficult. I don't know if I _____ (pass).

8 Write an idea for each of the statements (1–3).

1 a place I will visit in the next year

_____

2 something I am going to do in my studies or work

_____

3 an event I'm planning to go to

_____

9 Work in pairs. Take turns to tell each other the ideas that you wrote.

LISTENING 2

PRONUNCIATION FOR LISTENING

SOUNDING INTERESTED

1   When a speaker is bored or unhappy their voice goes down at the end. What happens if they are interested or happy?

really = The speaker is interested.

really = The speaker is not interested.

2   🔊 6.2 Listen to some sentences and answers. Write *I* (interested) or *B* (bored) for speaker B.

1   **A:** Did you know global warming is still increasing?
    B: Is it?   _____
2   **A:** It's my birthday today.
    B: Really? Happy birthday.   _____
3   **A:** The weather has got quite chilly hasn't it?
    B: I suppose so.   _____
4   **A:** Thanks for inviting me to your party!
    B: You're welcome. Be nice to see you!   _____
5   **A:** The dinner was lovely.
    B: Good. Glad you liked it.   _____

3   Work in pairs. Read the dialogues above out loud. Speaker B should change their intonation. Speaker A should guess whether Speaker B sounds interested or bored.

PREPARATION FOR LISTENING

4   Match the adjectives (1–8) to the adjectives with an opposite meaning (a–h). Use the glossary on page 203 to help you.

UNDERSTANDING
KEY VOCABULARY

1   happy   a   worst
2   warm   b   dry
3   best   c   calm
4   interested   d   energetic
5   exciting   e   unhappy
6   humid   f   cool, chilly
7   tired   g   bored
8   upset   h   dull

5 You are going to listen to a discussion between two students who have been asked to prepare a survey about the weather and how it changes people's moods. Choose the correct definition of a survey.

    1 a list of questions to help prepare for an exam on a specific topic
    2 a list of questions to ask different people to find out what they think

WHILE LISTENING

PRONUNCIATION FOR LISTENING

Recognizing mood

The way that people speak can help you understand their mood. Mood is the way that someone feels. When people speak their intonation tells you if they are happy and interested or upset and bored. Some listening exercises ask students to decide on the mood or opinion of the speaker.

UNLOCK
ONLINE

6 🔊 6.3 Listen to part 1 of the discussion and decide who is more interested in the work, Sergio or Murat.

7 🔊 6.3 Now listen again and complete the notes on the ideas map that Sergio wrote.

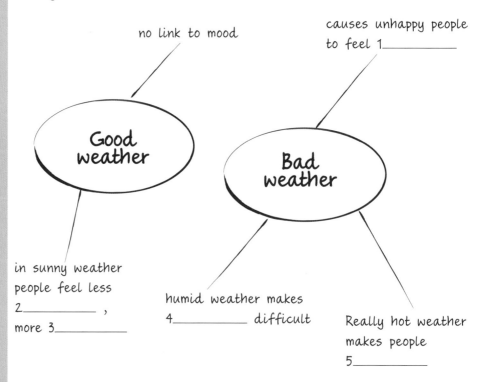

no link to mood

causes unhappy people to feel 1_____

Good weather

Bad weather

in sunny weather people feel less 2_____ , more 3_____

humid weather makes 4_____ difficult

Really hot weather makes people 5_____

8 Sergio and Murat have to choose the topic they think is the most important. Match the topics (1–4) with the reasons for choosing or not choosing it (a–d).

1 sunny weather (energy)
2 humid weather (work difficult)
3 bad weather (unhappy)
4 really hot weather (anger)

a wrong topic: not about feelings
b not sure if the facts are true
c final choice: Murat preferred it
d final choice: Murat didn't like it

9 Read the audioscript on page 217 to check your answers.

10 🔊 **6.4** Listen to the results of the survey in part 2. Choose the correct results.

1 *14 / 15* people prefer sunny weather to rainy weather.
2 *12 / 13* people could get more done when there was sunshine.
3 14 people said they have more energy when it is *light / dark*.
4 Sergio thinks the survey shows people have *more / less* energy when the weather is good.

DISCUSSION

11 Work in pairs. Discuss the questions.

1 Can you think of an example when weather has changed your mood?
2 Would it be easy for you to live in another country if the weather there was very different from the weather in your country?

CRITICAL THINKING

At the end of this unit you are going to do the speaking task below.

> Create and complete a survey about the use of land and how it affects the climate. Present the results of the survey to your classmates.

REMEMBER

1 You are going to study climate change in Africa and the Arctic. Work in pairs. What weather does Africa and the Arctic have? Make a list of how problems with the weather in these two countries affects people, animals and the environment.

2 Read the problems in the boxes below for Africa and the Arctic. Did you and your partner have the same ideas?

AFRICA

By 2050 up to 600 million people won't be able to get drinking water.

Drought will stop farmers growing food.

Shortage of clean water will help diseases to spread.

Some areas will be under the sea.

THE ARCTIC

The ice will melt.

Temperatures will go up more.

Sea levels will continue to rise.

Shortage of sea ice for polar bears and other animals to hunt.

Arctic wildlife begins to disappear.

EVALUATE

3 Write the phrases in the box in the gaps in the table (a–e) to complete the consequences. Use the glossary on page 203 to help you.

> People without drinking water   sea levels rise   disease will spread
> wildlife will begin to disappear   less food   temperatures rise more

causes of problem	consequence
Africa	
1 less rain falls	a People without drinking water
2 drought	b _____
3 less clean water	c _____
The Arctic	
4 ice will melt	d _____
5 less sea ice for animals to hunt from	e _____

4 Work in pairs. Compare your answers. Use the ideas from Exercise 3 which apply to the place you chose in Exercise 2.

Evaluating consequences

Using a consequence map can help you to organize your thoughts before a speaking task. Use your map to evaluate the possible effects of events or decisions.

5 Work in pairs. Look at the consequence map below for the Arctic. Create a consequence map for Africa using the ideas from Exercise 3 on page 117 and the empty boxes below. Add in arrows and more boxes if you need to.

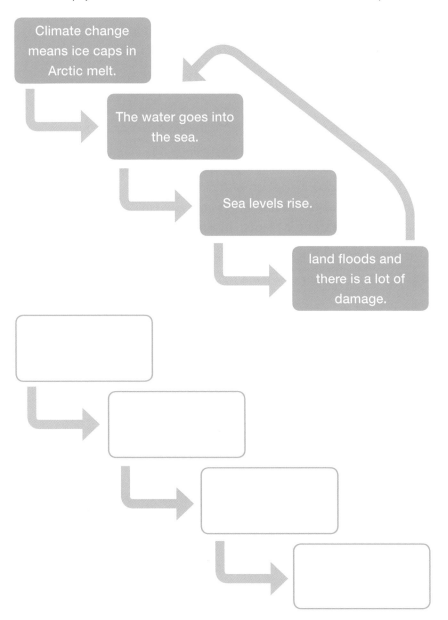

Climate change means ice caps in Arctic melt.

The water goes into the sea.

Sea levels rise.

land floods and there is a lot of damage.

6 Find a new partner and explain your ideas using your cause and consequence map to help you.

SPEAKING

PREPARATION FOR SPEAKING

PRONUNCIATION FOR SPEAKING

1 Decide which sentence in each of the pairs (a or b) is the cause and which is the consequence.

   1 **a** Our concentration drops.
      b It is more difficult to work in high humidity.
   2 **a** People feel more energetic in sunny weather.
      b They can get a lot of things done if the sun is shining.
   3 **a** There isn't enough water for plants, drinking and washing.
      b Some countries are very hot and don't get much rain.

2 🔊 **6.5** Listen to the sentences from Exercise 2 and write words in the gaps to complete the sentences.

   1 It is more difficult to work in high humidity _____ our concentration drops.
   2 People feel more energetic in sunny weather. _____ they can get a lot of things done if the sun is shining.
   3 Some countries are very hot and don't get much rain. _____ , there isn't enough water for plants, drinking and washing.

3 🔊 **6.6** Listen and repeat the linking words.

   1 so /səʊ/   **2** therefore /ðeəfɔ:/   **3** as a result /æzərɪzʌlt/

4 Work in pairs. Think of a consequence for each sentence. Be careful not to give a cause.

   1 The rainfall was too heavy.
      Therefore the village flooded. (consequence)
   2 The students didn't study much.
   3 A new factory was built in the city.
   4 Tigers are in danger of disappearing.
   5 Nowadays more people are interested in global warming.
   6 New cars are very expensive.
   7 Rainforests are getting smaller.
   8 I've lost my passport.
   9 Communication is much easier nowadays.

5 Choose four of the sentences and consequences you thought of in Exercise 4. Change the order of the sentences and this time explain the causes. Use *because of*, *because* and *due to*.

The village flooded (consequence) due to the heavy rainfall (cause).

6 Climate change is the consequence of burning fossil fuel. Look at the pictures and try to understand the process.

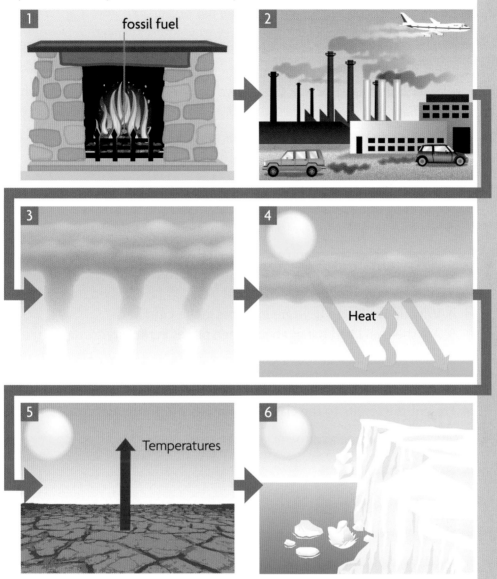

7 Work in pairs. Create a cause and consequence map to show how climate change can happen. Use the words in the box below and the glossary on page 203 to help you.

> burn   smoke   factory   gas(es)   trap heat
> ice   melt

8 Work in pairs. Describe the map together. Use some phrases from Exercises 3 and 5 to explain consequences and causes.

SPEAKING TASK

> Create and complete a survey about the use of land and how it affects the climate. Present the results of the survey to your classmates.

PREPARE

1 Work in groups of three or four. There is some land for sale in the centre of your home town or city. Create two consequence maps to show what could happen in each of the situations.

   1 The land becomes a park with trees and a lake.
   2 The land becomes factories and offices.

2 You want to find out what people in your class think should happen to the land by using a survey. Ask your classmates the questions and note down their answers to the following questions.

   1 Do you prefer the countryside or a city with factories? Why?
   2 What are the good things about having factories?
   3 What are the bad things?
   4 Why do we like to have green places in the city?
   5 Are there any bad things about green places in the city?

3 In your groups look at the results of the survey and make notes summarizing the information you have got.

PRESENT

4 Present the results to the class. Give causes and consequences.

TASK CHECKLIST	✔
Have you used collocations about weather and climate correctly?	
Have you used future forms correctly?	
Have you used sounds /ɒ/ and /əʊ/ correctly?	
Can you show interest when you respond?	
Can you link up sentences using so / therefore / as a result to show cause and consequence?	

OBJECTIVES REVIEW

I can ...

understand a film
about rain and the
water cycle.

| very well | not very well |

predict ideas from
research.

| very well | not very well |

use a cause and
consequence map.

| very well | not very well |

explain consequences.

| very well | not very well |

present the results of
a survey.

| very well | not very well |

WORDLIST

UNIT VOCABULARY		
as a result (phr)	exciting (adj)	prevent (v)
burn (v)	factory (n)	protect (v)
calm (adj)	flood (v)	rainfall (n)
chilly (adj)	foggy weather (phr)	rainforest (n)
climate change (phr)	forest (n)	sea levels (n)
cut down (v)	fossil fuel (phr)	smoke (n)
damage (v)	frog (n)	so (conj)
disappear (v)	gas (n)	species (n)
disease (n)	global warming (phr)	temperature (n)
drinking water (n)	humid (adj)	therefore (adv)
drought (n)	ice (n)	trap heat (phr)
dull (adj)	interested (adj)	wildlife (n)
energetic (adj)	melt (v)	

Watch and listen	Watch and understand a video about a famous horse race
Listening skills	Listen for bias; listen for corrections
Speaking skills	Ask for clarification; talk about advantages and disadvantages
Speaking task	Have a panel discussion about sport and money

London 2012

UNLOCK YOUR KNOWLEDGE

Work in pairs. Look at the photograph and answer the questions.

1 Which sport and event can you see in the photograph? Is this sport popular in your country?

2 Do you prefer to play individual or team sports? Why?

3 Do you like to win? Is it more important to win a competition or just to play a sport?

WATCH AND LISTEN

PREPARING TO WATCH

USING YOUR
KNOWLEDGE TO
PREDICT CONTENT

1 Work in pairs. Answer the questions.

    1 Have you ever seen a horse race in real life or on TV?
    2 Is horse racing popular in your country?

2 You are going to watch a video about a famous horse race. Make a list of the things you think you'll see in the video.

UNDERSTANDING
KEY VOCABULARY

3 Match the words (1–4) to the photographs (a–d).

    1 jockey
    2 town square
    3 banner
    4 racetrack

4 Match the words (1–7) to the definitions (a–g).

1 dangerous	**a** nervous or unhappy because of problems that
2 neighbourhood	may happen in the future
3 excited	**b** sad because something was not as good as you
4 fall	wanted or did not happen
5 lap	**c** happy because something good is going to
6 worried	happen
7 disappointed	**d** the place or area around your home
	e go down to the ground suddenly by accident
	f a complete journey around a track during a race
	g possibly bad or hurtful

5 Write a word from Exercise 4 in the gaps to complete the sentences.

1 Before I go to the dentist I always feel very _____ .

2 I am _____ if I don't pass an exam or test.

3 The _____ where I live is very friendly.

4 The day before my birthday I always feel very _____ .

5 Skydiving is a _____ hobby. You can get killed.

6 When the runner ran the last _____ of the race, the crowd shouted loudly.

7 Horses can _____ on the racetrack if the ground is wet.

6 Work in pairs. Discuss whether sentences 1–4 are true for you.

WHILE WATCHING

7 ▶ Watch the first two minutes of the video and tick the things that you see.

LISTENING FOR KEY INFORMATION

1 horses ☐
2 dogs ☐
3 guitars ☐
4 drums ☐
5 banners ☐
6 people running ☐
7 people singing ☐
8 a town square ☐
9 a town car park ☐
10 a racetrack ☐
11 a football pitch ☐

8 ▶ Watch the whole video. Answer the questions.

1 What is the Palio de Siena?
2 How many laps is it?
3 How many jockeys ride?
4 Why is Alberto happy to ride for Lupa?
5 What happens to Alberto?

DISCUSSION

9 Look at the sentence from the video and guess what the underlined words mean.

The city is <u>well-known</u> for its beautiful old buildings. It is also famous for the Palio di Siena horse race.

10 Work in pairs. Discuss whether there are any well-known places in your home town or city. What are they?

PREPARING TO LISTEN

1 Label the photograph with the words in the box. Use the glossary on page 205 to help you.

helmet   vest   gloves   competitor

a _____

b _____

c _____

d _____

2 Read the paragraph below and match the underlined words (1–5) to the definitions (a–e).

Most sports need a $^{(1)}$ <u>referee</u> to make sure that the $^{(2)}$ <u>score</u> is correct. Most sports are $^{(3)}$ <u>competitive</u> so it is important that people believe they are fair. In football, for example, you can $^{(4)}$ <u>kick</u> the ball but you can't $^{(5)}$ <u>hit</u> it with your hand. But there have been some famous matches where one of the players used his hand to get a goal and the referee did not see. People were very upset.

a use your foot quickly and hard to move something
b use your hand quickly and hard to move something
c a person who controls a match, checks the rules and counts the points
d describes an event where someone tries to win
e the number of points each person or team has in a game or match

3 Work in pairs. Discuss which of the underlined words in Exercise 2 can refer to taekwondo.

I think taekwondo is a competitive sport.

4 You are going to hear part of a panel discussion about Taekwondo. Choose the correct definition of a panel discussion.

   1 One person speaks about an idea in front of an audience and gives their opinion.
   2 Several people discuss an idea in front of an audience and show all the different opinions.
   3 Several people discuss an idea in front of an audience and try to agree on one opinion by the end.

Understanding bias

Before listening you should think about who is talking and why. Sometimes people are 'biased': they will have a special reason to agree or disagree with something. For example, a jockey will say horse racing is the most interesting sport but a footballer will choose football. So if you think about the person, this can give you information about what they might think before they speak. You can then listen for words that help you understand their opinions.

5 Match the person (1–3) to the statements (a–c).

   1 Someone who does taekwondo and loves it.
   2 Someone who hates taekwondo.
   3 Someone who is not sure about taekwondo.

   a Obviously taekwondo is boring.
   b Taekwondo is probably boring.
   c Actually taekwondo isn't boring at all.

WHILE LISTENING

6 During the panel discussion, the three people below talk about a plan to use a computer sensor in a Taekwondo vest to help with scoring. What do you think each person will feel about the new plan and why?

LISTENING FOR BIAS

   1 the Managing Director of Sports Technology Limited, the company which produces vest sensors
   2 an international taekwondo champion
   3 the head of the Referees Association

7 🔊 7.1 Listen to the discussion. Match the name of the person (a–c) with their job title in Exercise 6. Who agrees with the use of computer sensors in Taekwondo and who disagrees?

   a Nam Ki Gam
   b Raina Akintola
   c Sunan Wattana

8 🔊 **7.1** Listen again. Write *N* (Nam), *R* (Raina) and *S* (Sunan) next to their statements (1–6).

1 Obviously scoring was causing a lot of problems before. _____

2 ... in recent years, the scores have caused arguments because the referees have made mistakes. _____

3 Actually the scoring has worked well compared to other sports. _____

4 It also doesn't work if there is a kick to the head. So it definitely isn't needed. _____

5 Well, it probably won't cause any problems if we have a new system. _____

6 In the past, there have been times when the referee hasn't seen all the hits. _____

9 Check your answers with the audioscript on page 218.

DISCUSSION

10 Work in pairs. Discuss the questions.

1 Should technology be used in taekwondo?

2 What other sports use technology?

3 What problems do you think referees have in other sports?

4 What technology could be used for these problems?

⊙ LANGUAGE DEVELOPMENT

REVIEW OF THE PRESENT PERFECT

1 Put the words in sentences 1–6 from Listening 1 in the correct order.

1 brought / I've / one / to show you / here /.

2 In recent years / arguments / the scores / have caused / .

3 has / The scoring / to other sports / compared / worked well / .

4 problems / Has / caused / the scoring / before / ?

5 confuse / have / Competitors / tried to /them / .

6 tested / enough / The vest / hasn't been / .

2 Underline the Present perfect verb forms in Exercise 1. Does this tense connect the present with the future or the present with the past?

3 Look at sentences 4 and 6 in Exercise 1 again. Answer the questions.

1 In the question form, which is first: *have* or the subject?

2 In the negative form where does *not* go: before or after the verb *have*?

4 The Present perfect is used in three ways. Match the uses (1–3) to the time lines (a–c) in the box.

EXPLANATION

1 To talk about an action which finished in the past but which has a result now.

2 To talk about an action that started in the past and continues or is repeated now.

3 To talk about an experience in the past (could be at any time until now).

a _____

1 The vest hasn't been tested.
2 She's been to America to study.

past   ◆?   ◆?   ◆?   ◆?   ↓ now   future

b _____

1 I've brought one to show you.
2 Be careful. I've broken a glass: see!

past   ◆? - - - ◆   future
                        now

c _____

1 There have been arguments about scoring.
2 He's lived here for 12 years. He loves it.

past   ◆?~~~~~↓ now   future

5 Write the Present perfect form of the verb in brackets in the gaps to complete the sentences.

1 I'm not hungry because I ___'ve eaten___ (eat) breakfast already. (_1_)
2 _____ you ever _____ (use) a tablet before? (___)
3 My friend _____ (have) his watch for a long time. (___)
4 He's very dirty. He _____ just _____ (change) the wheels on his bike. (___)
5 How many English exams _____ you _____ (take) so far? (___)
6 It is cold in here. Someone _____ (open) the window. (___)
7 I _____ (visit) a lot of different countries. (___)
8 We _____ (not / meet) him before. This is the first time. (___)
9 Wow! You _____ already _____ (did) the housework. The house looks great! We can relax now! (___)
10 _____ you _____ (work) here for many years? (___)
11 I _____ (not / do) my homework yet so I can't watch TV. (___)

6 Match the sentences (1–11) in Exercise 5 to the uses (1–3) in Exercise 4.

6 🔊 **7.3** Listen again. Circle the mistake that Yasmin makes in each sentence. Then write the correct word.

1 In chess boxing they begin with boxing. _____

2 For urban golf you use golf clubs and a golf ball. _____

3 The Sahara Marathon happens over a week. _____

4 Sepak Takraw began in Indonesia. _____

POST-LISTENING

7 Write the phrases in the box in the gaps to complete the sentences that Yasmin used to correct her mistakes.

> sorry, I mean   or rather   no, not   well actually

1 They start with boxing- _____ chess.

2 You get clubs and a golf ball- _____ , it is a soft ball instead of a hard golf one.

3 This race is held every year over a week- _____ over six days.

4 The sport began in Indonesia and it- _____ Indonesia, it began in Malaysia.

8 Choose a popular sport. Write a sentence about the sport which has a factual mistake in it.

9 Work in pairs. Take turns to read your sentence from Exercise 8 out loud. Then correct it using the phrases in Exercise 7.

In football you need ten players. Well actually, you need eleven players, ten to play and a goalkeeper.

DISCUSSION

10 Work in small groups. Talk about which of the sports you would like to watch or try. Why?

CRITICAL THINKING

At the end of this unit you are going to do the speaking task below.

> Have a panel discussion about sport and money. Talk about advantages and disadvantages.

1 Work in pairs and answer the questions.

REMEMBER

1 What makes someone a good competitor?
2 What makes someone a good referee?
3 Do you think the best prize in a competition is always money?
4 Is it important for children to do activities where they can win or lose? If so why? If not, why not?
5 What other types of competition do we have in life?

2 Work in pairs. Decide which of the sentences (1–6) describe the advantages of playing urban golf and which describe the disadvantages.

APPLY

1 You don't need to go anywhere special.
2 You could break or damage something e.g. a window.
3 You don't need a lot of money.
4 You can wear anything you want.
5 You could argue with someone.
6 You could cause an accident e.g. hit a ball into a car.

Using ideas rakes

An ideas rake is designed to make sure you list at least five ideas. Using two ideas rakes for advantages and disadvantages gives you ten points to discuss and allows you to structure your responses in a discussion.

3 Work in pairs. Write the advantages from the list of sentences in Exercise 2 onto the ideas rake below. Then add two more advantages that you can think of.

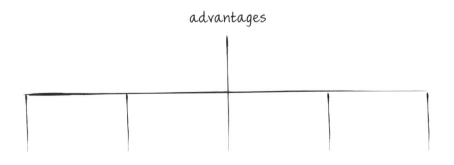

advantages

4 Write the disadvantages from the list of sentences in Exercise 2 onto the ideas rake below. Then add two more disadvantages that you can think of.

disadvantages

5 Choose one of the other sports from Listening 2. Make one ideas rake for the advantages and another for the disadvantages.

SPEAKING

PREPARATION FOR SPEAKING

UNL♦CK
ONLINE

1 Look at the sentences from Listening 2. Yasmin is talking about the advantages of different sports. Write the words in the gaps to complete the sentences.

thing   benefit   advantage   best

1 One _____ of this is that it tests people physically and mentally.

2 An _____ of urban golf is that you don't need to go anywhere special or need much money to play.

3 The _____ thing about it is that the winner can say he or she has won the hardest marathon in the world.

4 One good _____ about Sepak Takraw is that it is now played in schools in many countries including Canada.

UNL♦CK LISTENING AND SPEAKING SKILLS 2

2 Match each phrase to talk about disadvantages (a–d) to the phrases to talk about advantages in Exercise 1.

   a The worst thing about ... is ...
   b One bad thing about ... is ...
   c A disadvantage of... is ...
   d One drawback of this is ...

3 🔊 **7.4** Listen to the phrases. Which word in each phrase has the main stress? Underline the word.

   1 An advantage of this is _____ .
   2 A disadvantage of this is _____ .
   3 A benefit of this is _____ .
   4 A problem with this is _____ .
   5 The best thing about this is _____ .
   6 The worst thing about this is _____ .
   7 One good thing is _____ .
   8 One bad thing is _____ .

4 🔊 **7.4** Listen again and repeat.

5 Write the ideas from the rakes from pages 133 and 134 in the gaps in Exercise 3 above to complete the sentences about the sport you chose.

6 Work in pairs with someone who chose the same sport as you in Exercise 5 on page 134. Discuss the advantages and disadvantages you wrote about. Did you have similar ideas?

7 Work in pairs. Discuss the questions.

   1 The photograph shows a Sepak Takraw competitor. What do you think the rules of the game are?
   2 Do you think it's important to have rules in sport? Why / why not?

8 An interviewer is speaking to a Sepak Takraw competitor. Number the sentences in the correct order.

    a I: *What do you mean by Tekong?*   _____

    b C: Yes, I thought we played well. We made a few silly mistakes though.   _____

    c C: That's the player who serves the ball during the match ...   _____

    d I: Which mistakes did you make? *Can you go into a bit more detail about this.*   _____

    e C: Yes, sure. I thought that the ball went outside the court too much. Also, our Tekong jumped off the ground once or twice.   _____

    f I: Did you enjoy the game?   _1_

9 Look at the words in italics in Exercise 8. They show ways of asking a person to explain more. Can you think of others ways to ask?

10 Look at the phrases below. Write *DU* (I don't understand) and *EM* (I want you to explain more).

    1 Sorry I don't follow.   _____

    2 Can you explain what you mean?   _____

    3 I'm afraid I didn't get that.   _____

    4 I'm sorry but I don't understand.   _____

    5 Would you mind giving me some examples?   _____

11 Work in groups of three. You are going to plan a sports competition to encourage people to use your local sports centre. Follow steps 1–4.

    1 Choose a popular sport or activity for your competition.

    2 Decide where the competition will be held and the equipment you'll need.

    3 Think of reasons why people would / wouldn't want to take part in the competition.

    4 Decide together on a prize to give to the winner of the competition.

12 Work in pairs with someone from the other group. Follow steps 1–3.

    1 Take turns to explain your competitions to each other.

    2 Ask each other for more information if you don't understand.

    3 Choose the competition you think will work best.

SPEAKING TASK

> Have a panel discussion about sport and money. Talk about advantages and disadvantages.

1 Work in pairs. Think of three advantages and disadvantages of sportsmen and sportswomen getting paid a lot of money.

2 Write notes in the two ideas rakes below. Use the advantages and disadvantages you thought of in Exercise 1.

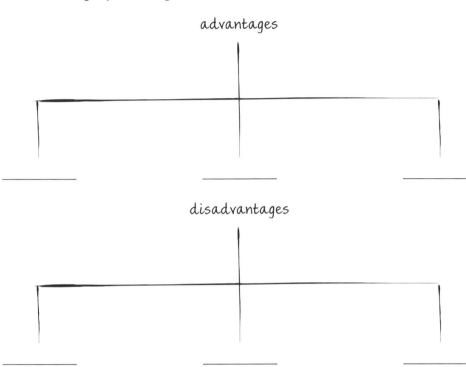

advantages

disadvantages

3 Work in groups of four. Read your role card on page 195 (Student A), 197 (Student B) or 198 (Students C and D). Prepare for the panel discussion.

4 Have the panel discussion in your roles. Student D should start. Remember to talk about advantages and disadvantages. Ask for clarification if you need to.

TASK CHECKLIST	✔
Have you used Present perfect correctly?	
Have you understood vocabulary to talk about sport?	
Have you used weak forms and elided sounds correctly?	
Have you asked for clarification using the correct language?	

OBJECTIVES REVIEW

I can ...

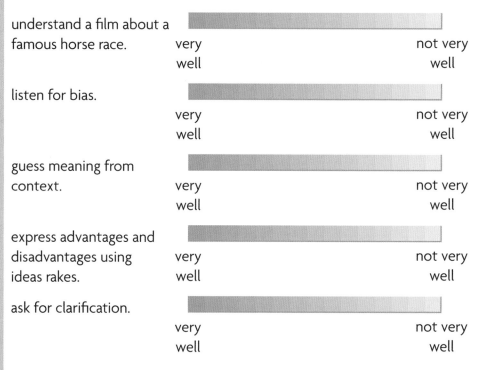

understand a film about a famous horse race.

very well   not very well

listen for bias.

very well   not very well

guess meaning from context.

very well   not very well

express advantages and disadvantages using ideas rakes.

very well   not very well

ask for clarification.

very well   not very well

WORDLIST

UNIT VOCABULARY	
actually (adv)	helmet (n)
advantage (n)	hit (v)
already (adv)	ice skating (n)
benefit (n)	just (adv)
best (adj)	kick (v)
board (n)	lose (v)
boxing (n)	medal (n)
chess (n)	obviously (adv)
club (n)	piece (n)
compete (v)	pitch (n)
competition (n)	player (n)
competitive (adj)	prize (n)
competitor (n)	probably (adv)
course (n)	racquet (n)
court (n)	referee (n)
cup (n)	ring (n)
definitely (adv)	rink (n)
disadvantage (n)	score (n)
ever (adv)	skate (n)
football (n)	tennis (n)
game (n)	vest (n)
glove (n)	worst (adj)
goal (n)	yet (adv)
golf (n)	

LEARNING OBJECTIVES

Watch and listen	Watch and understand a video about South African Cape fishermen
Listening skills	Recognize numbers; listen for reaction
Speaking skills	Learn phrases for giving advice
Speaking task	Give advice to solve work or study problems

UNL⭕CK YOUR KNOWLEDGE

Work in pairs. Look at the photograph and answer the questions.

1 What type of job do you think the person in the photograph is doing?
2 Could you work in an office like this?
3 What kind of job would you do if money wasn't important?
4 What are the advantages and disadvantages of working?

WATCH AND LISTEN

PREPARING TO WATCH

1 You are going to watch a video about fishermen. Look at the four
photographs from the video and the map. Work with a partner and
answer the questions.

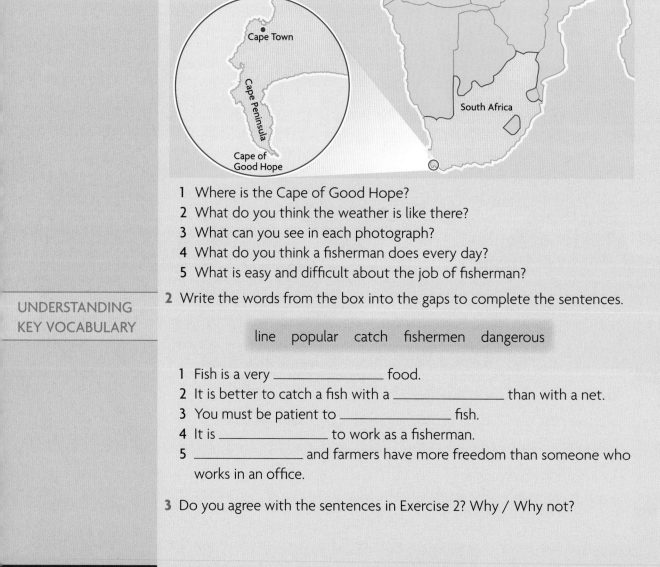

1 Where is the Cape of Good Hope?
2 What do you think the weather is like there?
3 What can you see in each photograph?
4 What do you think a fisherman does every day?
5 What is easy and difficult about the job of fisherman?

2 Write the words from the box into the gaps to complete the sentences.

> line   popular   catch   fishermen   dangerous

1 Fish is a very _____ food.
2 It is better to catch a fish with a _____ than with a net.
3 You must be patient to _____ fish.
4 It is _____ to work as a fisherman.
5 _____ and farmers have more freedom than someone who
   works in an office.

3 Do you agree with the sentences in Exercise 2? Why / Why not?

WHILE WATCHING

4 ▶ Watch the video. Choose the correct word to complete the notes.

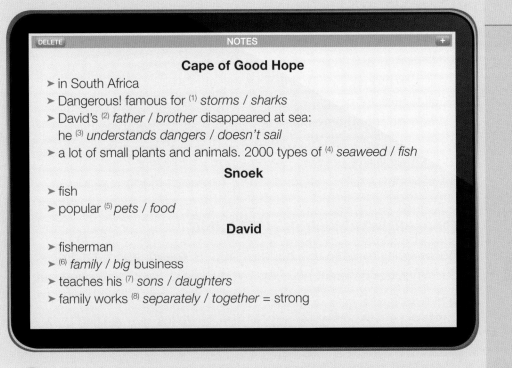

DELETE | NOTES | +

Cape of Good Hope
➤ in South Africa
➤ Dangerous! famous for (1) *storms / sharks*
➤ David's (2) *father / brother* disappeared at sea:
  he (3) *understands dangers / doesn't sail*
➤ a lot of small plants and animals. 2000 types of (4) *seaweed / fish*

Snoek
➤ fish
➤ popular (5) *pets / food*

David
➤ fisherman
➤ (6) *family / big* business
➤ teaches his (7) *sons / daughters*
➤ family works (8) *separately / together* = strong

5 ▶ Match the sentence halves. Then watch the video again and check.

1 The Cape of Good Hope is dangerous because …
2 The Cape is a good place for fishermen because …
3 David has to be patient because …
4 The Snoek are difficult to find because …
5 David has to be careful because …
6 David is lucky today because …

a the Snoek are dangerous.
b it has 2000 types of fish.
c he has more than 300 fish.
d the Snoek are difficult to find.
e storms can sink ships there.
f they look for food in different places.

DISCUSSION

6 Work in pairs and answer the questions.

1 Would you like a job connected to the sea?
2 Would you like to work in a job that isn't in an office?

PREPARING TO LISTEN

1 Choose the correct words in italics to show the meaning of the words in bold.

1 We **earn** money by *working / saving it.*
2 **Colleagues** are people who are *in our family / we work with.*
3 When we **spend time** on something it means *we pay for it / use time doing it.*
4 When we **waste time** we *use time badly / are late.*
5 A **project** is a *special place to work / piece of planned work.*

PRONUNCIATION FOR LISTENING

2 You are going to listen to a business student speaking about a project which includes different numbers. Work in pairs. Say the numbers out loud.

1 48%   2 ½   3 ⅓   4 31.5   5 103   6 1,540   7 6,001

3 🔊 8.1 Listen, check and repeat.

4 Work in pairs. Answer the questions.

1 Do we say *and* after *a thousand* or after *a hundred*?
2 What is another way to say ½ using %?
3 Can we use *a* with *half / third / quarter* etc.?
5 How do we say *0* when it is in a decimal number e.g. *0.5* ?
6 How do we say *0* when it is in a longer set of information e.g. *0044 1789 830* ?

WHILE LISTENING

Understanding numbers

Numbers are difficult to hear if they are said quickly or if they are very long. You need to understand the numbers but also any words related to numbers e.g. *per cent; point.* Practise listening and writing numbers as much as you can.

5 (◀))8.2 Listen to a conversation between a university professor and a student. Decide if the sentences (1–5) are true or false.

1 Alika has finished her research and is ready to give it to the professor.
2 She read a lot of reports.
3 She looked at why people like or dislike their jobs.
4 People waste time at work by surfing the internet, talking to other people and taking long breaks.
5 A lot of people wasted time at work because they hated their manager and didn't want to work for him / her.

6 (◀))8.2 Listen again and complete the information on the chart below.

RECOGNIZING
NUMBERS

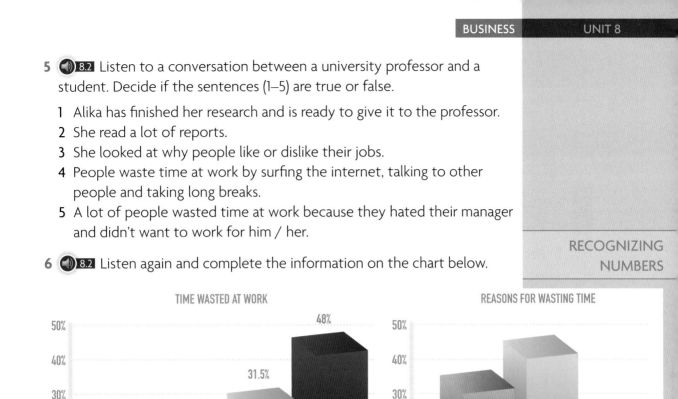

TIME WASTED AT WORK

REASONS FOR WASTING TIME

DISCUSSION

7 Work in pairs. You are the managers of a company. Choose two ideas from the list (1–4) that you think will stop people wasting time at work.

1 Make sure everyone has a regular break.
2 Pay a very high wage.
3 Shout at people who waste time.
4 Give extra pay to people who work fast.

8 Decide whether you agree or disagree with the sentences.

1 Earning a lot of money is more important than having an interesting job.
2 The most exciting work is to have your own business.
3 Younger people do not have enough experience to be good managers.
4 Older people with families don't work as hard as young, single people.
5 People who work the longest hours do the most work.
6 The best time to start work is after university.

9 Work in pairs. Compare your answers to Exercise 8.

MULTI-WORD VERBS

7 Multi-word verbs have more than one part: a verb and a particle, or particles. Underline the multi-word verbs from Listening 1 in the sentences.

> 1 You have <u>noted</u> a lot of information <u>down</u>.
>
> 2 I haven't finished yet- I ran out of time.
>
> 3 I noted down the key information.
>
> 4 I took part in the discussions on this.
>
> 5 I found out a large amount of information.
>
> 6 I found a lot of interesting information out.
>
> 7 I looked at how people spend time at work ...
>
> 8 ... the reasons why they didn't get on with their work
>
> 9 They only just had enough money to get by.

8 Write the infinitive form of the multi-word verbs from Exercise 7 next to their definition in the table. Then check your answers with the glossary on page 206.

verb	definition
1	to use all of something or there isn't enough of it
2	to continue to do something (especially work)
3	to get information for the first time
4	to be able to live with difficulty, usually by having just enough of what you need
5	to make or write a note
6	to do an activity with other people
7	to read or think about something carefully

9 Write the sentences from Exercise 7 in the gaps to complete the rules about multi-word verbs.

EXPLANATION

1 Multi-word verbs can be used with objects. Sometimes the object goes **either** between the verb and the particle **or** after the verb and the particle.

verb + object + particle

You have noted a lot of information down.

(1) _____

verb + particle + object

(2) _____

(3) _____

2 Sometimes the object **only** goes after the verb and the particle. When this happens the multi-word verb is 'inseparable'.

verb + particle + object

I ran out of time.

(4) _____

(5) _____

(6) _____

3 Some multi-word verbs don't take an object. When this happens, the multi-word verb is 'intransitive'.

A third of people only just had enough money to get by.

10 Check you understand the meaning of the multi-word verbs below. Use the glossary on page 206 to help you. Then match them to the grammar rules in the box (1–3).

1 She looks after my children when I am at work.
2 She decided to take yoga up to help with stress.
3 I need to leave the meeting early, but you can carry on.

11 Match the sentence halves. Use the multi-word verbs in bold to help you.

1 Would you like to **take**	a **up** a new hobby? If so what would you do?
2 Can you **get**	b **after** children? Why / Why not?
3 If you have to **find**	c **on** with your work if it's noisy?
4 Do you **note**	d **out** new information for a lesson where do you look?
5 Have you ever **run out**	e **of** money while you were out? How did you **get by**?
6 Is it easy to **look**	f **down** phone numbers or put them straight into your phone?

12 Work in pairs. Ask and answer the questions in Exercise 11.

PREPARING TO LISTEN

1 Match the words (1–8) with their opposites (a–h).

1	anxious	a	short term
2	long term	b	happy
3	strengths	c	careless
4	practice test	d	calm
5	excellent	e	real test
6	careful	f	weaknesses
7	upset	g	bad
8	smart	h	untidy

2 Work in pairs. Answer the questions.

Can you think of:
1 a strength you have and a weakness you have?
2 something that makes you feel upset?
3 the last time you did a practice exam or test?
4 a long term plan you have?
5 someone you know who is careless?
6 someone you know who is calm?
7 someone who always looks smart?
8 a time when you got an excellent grade for a piece of work?

3 You are going to listen to a mentor talking to Sami, a student. The mentor has been giving Sami advice. Work in pairs. Discuss these questions.

1 Look at the photograph. Which person is the mentor?
2 Would you like to get advice from a mentor? Why / Why not?
3 Would you like to be a mentor? Do you think you would be good at it? Why / Why not?
4 Do you think practice interviews are useful or not? Why? / Why not?

WHILE LISTENING

LISTENING FOR
REACTION

4 🔊 **8.3** Listen to the dialogue. Tick the advice that the mentor gives Sami about what he should do in an interview.

1 Keep calm and listen carefully. ☐
2 Speak a lot. ☐
3 Give lots of detail. ☐
4 Take examples of work. ☐

5 Smile and be positive. ☐
6 Answer confidently. ☐
7 Make eye contact. ☐
8 Dress smartly. ☐

UNLOCK ONLINE

5 🔊 **8.4** Listen to the first part of the dialogue again and number the phrases below in the order you hear them.

a Why was it useful   ____
b Enjoy it... No not really   ____
c Did you enjoy it   ____
d But you remember some of the questions   ____
e Oh yes   ____

6 Work in pairs. Decide which of the sentences in Exercise 5 look like statements and which sentences look like questions.

7 🔊 **8.5** Listen to sentence e in Exercise 5. Does it sound like a statement or question? Why?

8 🔊 **8.6** Listen to the sentences in Exercise 5 again and repeat.

POST-LISTENING

9 Work in pairs. Put the words in the correct order to make questions the mentor asked Sami in the interview.

1 Why / work with / like / would you / to / us / ?
2 What / your strengths / are / and weaknesses / ?
3 Why / the job / we give / should / you / ?
4 What / you / long term / ? / do / want / to do
5 Are / always / you / on time / ?
6 Are / good at / in a team / working / you / ?
7 What / qualifications / kind of / you / have / got / ?
8 When / a difficult problem / did / solve / you last / ?

DISCUSSION

10 Work in pairs. Discuss the questions.

1 Do you think you are good at interviews? Why / Why not?
2 Do you think you are good at giving advice? Why / Why not?

PREPARATION FOR SPEAKING

UNLOCK ONLINE

1 Choose one of the categories (a–c) which describes the function of this sentence.

If you want to do better, you should start by looking more confident.

a explaining
b requesting
c giving advice

2 Which of the phrases are also ways of introducing advice?

1 I can help you.
2 I think you should ...
3 Be careful not to ...
4 Do you want to ...
5 Shall we ...?
6 Why don't you ...?

3 Work in pairs. Look at the picture of a student called JP. Think of reasons why he can't find a job.

4 Work in pairs. Complete the sentences (1–5) with advice to give JP.

1 If I were you, I would …

_____ .

2 I think you should …

_____ .

3 If you want to do better, you should …

_____ .

4 Be careful not to …

_____ .

5 You should try (not) to …

_____ .

5 Read a conversation between JP and his teacher. Underline the advice that the teacher gives.

Teacher: I think you should try to work a bit harder JP.
JP: Oh.
Teacher: Yes. I don't want to upset you but you don't do enough work at the moment.
JP: Ok. I understand what you are saying. I'll try to work harder.
Teacher: And if you want to do better, you need to complete more project work.
JP: Do I?
Teacher: I know it's difficult but at least you know what you need to do.
JP: Ok, then.

6 Work in pairs. Student A: turn to page 195. Student B: turn to page 197.

7 Imagine you are a mentor. Work in groups of three. Make a list of ten dos and don'ts of finding a job which are useful for everyone.

8 Find someone from another group and take it in turns to give advice.

SPEAKING TASK

> Think of some solutions to a work or study problem and give advice to someone.

PREPARE

1 Work in pairs. Look at the list of study and work problems (1–5). Think of two or three solutions for each problem. Use the words and phrases in the box and a dictionary to help you.

> get lots of rest   make a timetable   talk to someone   ask for help
> discuss it with your teacher   ask for advice   go to bed early
> be friendly   study for short periods   use a calendar   try to concentrate
> write notes for yourself   write a 'to do' list   relax   don't give up!

1 working / studying long hours
2 not getting on with a boss or classmate
3 not enjoying your job or studies
4 finding it difficult to organize time
5 finding it difficult to do enough work or study

2 Choose two problems from Exercise 1.

DISCUSS

3 Work with three different partners. Take turns to ask each person about the problems they chose in Exercise 2 and to give them advice.

TASK CHECKLIST	✔
Can you say numbers correctly?	
Have you used comparatives and multi-word verbs correctly?	
Have you used ways of giving advice?	

OBJECTIVES REVIEW

I can ...

understand a video about cape fishermen.

very well · not very well

listen for numbers.

very well · not very well

listen for people's reactions.

very well · not very well

assess qualities for work using a cluster diagram.

very well · not very well

give advice.

very well · not very well

WORDLIST

UNIT VOCABULARY		
anxious (adj)	find out (v)	real (adj)
apprentice (n)	get by (v)	run out of (v)
bad (adj)	get on with (v)	ship (n)
best (adj)	half (n)	single (adj)
boring (adj)	job title (n)	sink (v)
business (n)	learn (v)	smart (adj)
calm (adj)	look at (v)	spend time (phr)
careful (adj)	manager (n)	storm (n)
careless (adj)	note down (v)	take part (v)
carry on with (v)	percent (n)	take up (v)
driving licence (n)	personal quality (n)	untidy (adj)
earn (v)	point (v)	upset (adj)
excellent (adj)	practice (n)	worst (adj)
experience (n)	qualification (n)	

LEARNING OBJECTIVES

Watch and listen	Watch and understand a video about internet inventors
Listening skills	Listen for attitude; listen for detail
Speaking skills	Talk about an object's appearance and functions
Speaking task	Describe an object and its functions

UNLOCK YOUR KNOWLEDGE

Work in pairs. Look at the photograph and answer the questions.

1 Some people are extraordinary: they do very special, unusual or strange things. Do you know anyone like this?

2 Why is the person in the picture extraordinary? What kind of character do extraordinary people have?

3 What extraordinary thing would you like to do?

⊙ LANGUAGE DEVELOPMENT

-ED AND -ING ADJECTIVES

UNLOCK
ONLINE

1 Look at the sentences from Listening 1. Underline the adjectives in each one.

> 1 That is amazing!
>
> 2 Why are you interested in him?
>
> 3 He was a fascinating man.
>
> 4 Are you bored?

2 Compare the two sentences (a and b). Underline the word that the adjective describes.

1 a The <u>news</u> was surprising.
   b <u>I</u> was surprised by the news.
2 a I was always bored when I went to see her.
   b She was boring so I tried not to see her.
3 a He was excited by the idea for the new business.
   b His idea for the new business was exciting.
4 a The man was very interested in my story.
   b The man told me a very interesting story.
5 a The walk was very tiring.
   b The walk took a long time because I was tired.
6 a What a fascinating picture!
   b My friend was fascinated by the picture but I didn't like it.

3 Write *-ed* or *-ing* in the gaps to complete the rules in the box.

EXPLANATION

1 Adjectives ending in _____ describe the reason for a feeling e.g. a situation or thing.

2 Adjectives ending in _____ describe what people feel as the result of something.

4 Work in pairs. Take turns to tell each other an example of each situation (1–6).

1 an exciting hobby
2 an interesting person you know
3 what makes you feel very tired
4 the last time a book or video fascinated you
5 the last time you were bored
6 a boring job

SUFFIXES

5 Choose the correct option in each sentence to complete the rules in the box.

EXPLANATION

1 Suffixes come at the *beginning / end* of a word.

2 The suffixes *-ing* and *-ed* often make words into *nouns / adjectives*.

6 Write the adjective form of the verbs and nouns (Column A) in the column with the correct suffix to complete the tables.

A	Adjectives			
Verbs	-ing	-ed	-able	-ful
excite	exciting	excited	excitable	—
surprise			—	—
believe	—	—		—
succeed	—	—	—	
comfort				—
relax			—	—
shock				—

Nouns	-ive	-e	-y
expense		—	—
happiness	—	—	
politeness	—		—

7 Look at the answers in the tables again and answer the questions.

1 Which verbs and nouns end in *-e*?

2 What happens to the spelling of the verb or noun ending in *-e* when the adjective is formed?

3 What happens to the *-i* in the word *happiness* when forming an adjective?

8 Read the text about Joseph Conrad quickly. What was his job and why was he an extraordinary person?

9 Write the correct form of the words in brackets in the gaps to complete the text.

Joseph Conrad was born in 1857 in Ukraine. His father was a writer and translator of famous books and plays. Joseph read these books and became (1)_____ (fascinate) with literature. Joseph's family were rich but he didn't have a very (2)_____ (happiness) childhood. Because of his parents' political beliefs, he and his family had to move to Northern Russia where life was very hard. Both Joseph's parents died when he was only twelve years old. But then there was a (3)_____ (surprise) change to his luck. Joseph's uncle decided to look after him and to pay for an (4)_____ (expense) education in Latin, Greek,

Geography and Mathematics. Unfortunately, Joseph didn't enjoy lessons. Instead, he told his uncle that he wanted to become a sailor and to travel to Africa by ship. Joseph enjoyed having adventures at sea and meeting lots of (5)_____ (interest) people. These people were later included in his books. After he retired from sailing, Joseph bought a house in England and in 1895, he wrote his first book, *Almayer's Folly*. Many more books followed and Joseph Conrad became one of the most (6)_____ (success) 20th century novelists. His most famous book is perhaps *Heart of Darkness*. One of the reasons his books were popular was that the characters and situations he wrote about were very (7)_____ (believe).

LISTENING 2

PREPARING TO LISTEN

1 Match the shapes to the nouns in the box.

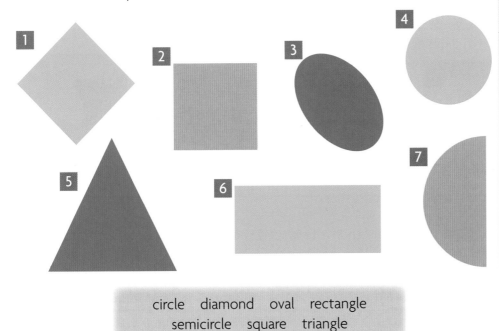

```
circle   diamond   oval   rectangle
   semicircle   square   triangle
```

2 Work in pairs. Say the nouns in Exercise 1 out loud and underline the stressed syllable in each word.

3 Underline the nouns and circle the adjectives connected with shape in the sentences (1–5).

　1 Name two things that are round, rectangular, triangular, oval and square.
　2 Which shape does two semicircles make?
　3 Which shapes make two triangles if you divide them into two parts?
　4 Are road signs usually circular, square or diamond-shaped in your country?
　5 Draw a line on each shape in Exercise 1 to make two halves.

4 Work in pairs. Answer the question.

Which nouns lose *e* or *le* and have *-ular* added to make an adjective form? Which are exceptions?

5 Where is the stress in each adjective form? Is it the same as the nouns?

6 Work in pairs and answer the questions in Exercise 3.

WHILE LISTENING

7 🔊 **9.3** Listen and write the name of the invention (1–4) and the inventor
(a–c) under the correct photograph.

1 hand-dryer
2 egg chair
3 wheelbarrow
4 climbing car

a James Dyson
b Roman Mistiuk
c Arne Jacobsen

_____   _____   _____   _____
_____   _____   _____   _____

8 🔊 **9.3** Listen again and write a word in each gap to complete the
student's notes.

invention	what it looks like	advantages / disadvantages
chair	It's (1)_____ and comes in lots of different (2)_____ .	Advantage: beautiful design Disadvantage: Probably not very (3)_____
wheelbarrow	Has (4)_____ parts: a (5)_____ frame and a round wheel	Advantage: Wheel shape allows it to move (6)_____ . Disadvantage: Probably more (7)_____ than other wheelbarrows.
hand-dryer	Has one big single part- it is long and (8)_____ from the front.	Advantage: dries hands (9)_____: no need to use towels or to touch buttons Disadvantage: relies on electricity
climbing car	It's (10)_____-shaped with plastic or glass sides and roof.	Advantage: saves (11)_____ Disadvantage: not able to climb all types of (12)_____

DISCUSSION

9 Work in small groups. Discuss the questions.

1 Which of the inventions do you think is best and why?
2 Do you think design can help improve life for people?
3 Which 'ordinary' things are actually special and help us?

CRITICAL THINKING

At the end of this unit you are going to do the speaking task below.

> Describe an object. Talk about what it looks like and its functions.
> Consider its advantages and disadvantages.

1 Work with a partner. Answer the questions about objects you use.

   1 How many objects do you use every day? Which ones?
   2 Which objects are most important to you? Why?
   3 Did you buy these objects or were they given to you? Why?
   4 Which objects would you like to own in the future?

Description wheel

Use a description wheel to quickly record different aspects of a topic. Write brief notes in each section to organize your presentation.

2 Write the words from the box in the correct sections of the description wheel below.

> plastic   large   flat   expensive   heavy   black
> to provide entertainment   glass   rectangular   ~~internet display~~
> to provide information   high definition   1m wide

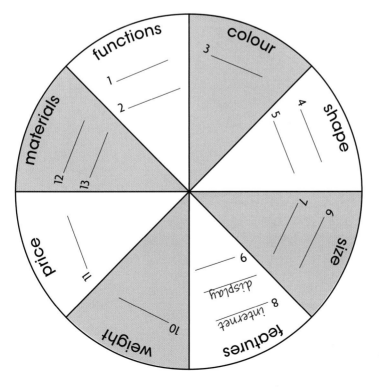

3 Which object is described in the wheel?

4 Look at the picture of a mechanical torch. Correct the words in *italics* in the description.

The mechanical torch is made of plastic and glass. It is not heavy, it is light. It has ⁽¹⁾ *five* parts: a handle and the main body. It is ⁽²⁾ *circle* at the front and there is a small ⁽³⁾ *square* glass part at the front for the light. On the side there is a handle which you can pull out. This is ⁽⁴⁾ *short* and thin. It is used to wind up the torch to give it power.

5 Complete the description wheel with words and phrases from the description in Exercise 4

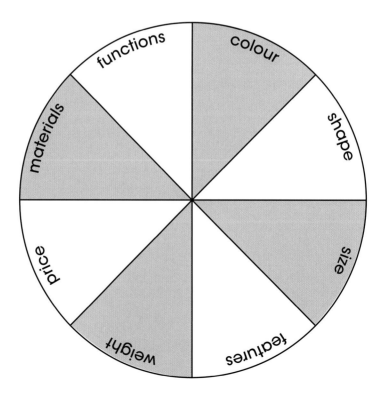

6 Work in pairs. Discuss the advantages and disadvantages of the mechanical torch and make notes in the table. Use the ideas below.

- electricity
- being in a car
- how easy it is to start
- using it when tired
- size

invention	
advantages	disadvantages

7 Work in pairs to describe photographs of objects to your partner. Student A go to page 195 and read the instructions. Student B, go to page 198 and read the instructions

SPEAKING

PREPARATION FOR SPEAKING

1 Match the headings (1–6) in Column A to the information about a mechanical radio in Column B.

A	B
1 name of the object	a the mechanical radio
2 what it is made of	b People with no electricity can still use the wind up radio so they can communicate and get information about the rest of the world.
3 the different parts of the object	c plastic and metal
4 what it is used for	d It can only work for a short time; the radios are still expensive for poor people.
5 advantages	e It helps poor people; it works everywhere and in every situation.
6 disadvantage	f two main parts: the body of the radio and a handle to wind the radio. It also has a solar panel and antennae.

2 Write one word in each gap to complete the description of the radio in the diagram. Use the information (a–f) below to help you.

a *is used for* + verb-*ing*   d *lets* + subject + verb (infinitive)
b *is a thing for* + verb-*ing*   e *is made of* + noun
c *is used to* + verb (infinitive) f *has ... main parts.*

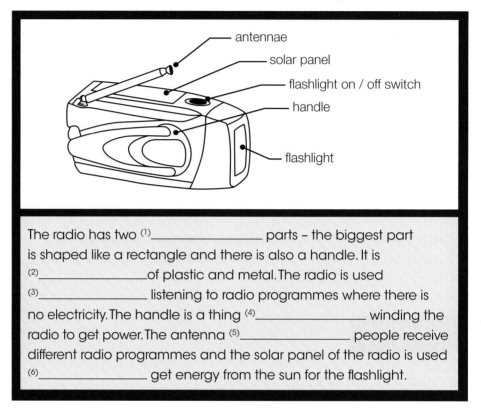

antennae
solar panel
flashlight on / off switch
handle
flashlight

The radio has two (1)_____ parts – the biggest part
is shaped like a rectangle and there is also a handle. It is
(2)_____of plastic and metal. The radio is used
(3)_____ listening to radio programmes where there is
no electricity. The handle is a thing (4)_____ winding the
radio to get power. The antenna (5)_____ people receive
different radio programmes and the solar panel of the radio is used
(6)_____ get energy from the sun for the flashlight.

3 Write answers to the questions (1–5) about the radio above. Use the description in Exercise 3 to help you.

1 What's it made of?

_____

2 What does it look like?

_____

3 What's it used for?

_____

4 What does the antennae let you do?

_____

5 What is the solar panel used to do?

_____

PRONUNCIATION FOR SPEAKING

4 Look at the words in bold in the questions and answers (1–5). What happens to the sound of the second word in the answers?

1 a What's it **made of**?
   /meɪdɒv/

b It's **made of** plastic and metal.
   /meɪdəv/

2 a What's it **used for**?
   /juːzdfɔː/

b It's **used for** playing a radio without electricity.
   /juːzdfə/

3 a What is this thing **used for**?
   /juːzdfɔ/

b It's a thing **used for** winding the radio up.
   /juːzdfə/

4 a What is this part **used to** do?
   /juːztʊ/

b It's **used to** do the winding.
   /juːztʊ/

5 a What does this part let you do?

b It lets you find different channels.

5 🔊 9.4 Listen to the questions and answers and repeat.

6 Work in pairs. Write the names of the objects in the photographs.

7 Work in groups of three. Student A: choose an object but don't tell your group what it is. Students B and C ask student A some questions and find the object. Take it in turns to choose the object.

B: What does it look like?
A: It has two parts: the main part is round and there is a handle.
C: What's it made of?
A: It's usually made of metal or plastic.
B: What's it used for?
A: It's used for cleaning: the handle is used to carry it.
C: Is it the bucket?

1 _____
2 _____
3 _____
4 _____
5 _____
6 _____
7 _____
8 _____
9 _____
10 _____

SPEAKING TASK

> Describe an object. Talk about what it looks like and its functions.
> Consider its advantages and disadvantages.

PREPARE

1 Work in pairs and choose an object. Make notes in the table below.

Object	
1 name of the object	
2 what it is made of	
3 the different parts of the object	
4 what it is used for	
5 advantages	
6 disadvantages	

DISCUSS

2 Work with another pair. Take turns to tell each other about the object you and your partner chose. Don't tell the other pair the name of the object. See if they can guess it. When you are listening, ask questions about the object to help you find the answer.

TASK CHECKLIST	✔
Can you use words and intonation to sound less negative and more positive?	
Can you use –ed and –ing adjectives correctly?	
Can you use suffixes to change a word's class?	
Can you use phrases to describe the appearance and functions of an object?	

OBJECTIVES REVIEW

I can ...

listen for attitude.

very well   not very well

describe and evaluate useful objects.

very well   not very well

talk about the appearance and functions of an object.

very well   not very well

present and describe an object.

very well   not very well

WORDLIST

UNIT VOCABULARY		
bag (n)	headphones (n)	remarkable (adj)
believable (adj)	homeless (adj)	round (adj)
belt (n)	interesting / interested (adj)	ruler (n)
boring / bored (adj)		semicircle (n)
broom (n)	invent (v)	shocked / shocking (adj)
bucket (n)	invention (n)	
circular (adj)	lamp (n)	square (n)
comb (n)	length (n)	successful (adj)
comfortable (adj)	made of (phr)	surprised / surprising (adj)
diamond-shaped (adj)	metal (n)	
emperor (n)	mug (n)	sword (n)
exciting / excited (adj)	oval (adj) (n)	tiring / tired (adj)
expensive (adj)	plastic (n)	triangular (adj)
extraordinary (adj)	polite (adj)	used to (v)
fascinating / fascinated (adj)	rectangle (n)	weight (n)
	rectangular (adj)	wheelbarrow (n)
funeral (n)	relaxed / relaxing (adj)	wind (v)
handle (n)		

LEARNING OBJECTIVES

Watch and listen	Watch and understand a video about space
Listening skills	Use context to guess words; listen to an introduction
Speaking skills	Using body language to show interest; turn-taking
Speaking task	Plan a conference about space exploration

UNL⊘CK YOUR KNOWLEDGE

Work in pairs. Look at the photograph and answer the questions.

1 What do the photographs show?
2 Would you like to visit another planet one day?
3 Do you think we should spend a lot of money on space exploration? Why / Why not?

WATCH AND LISTEN

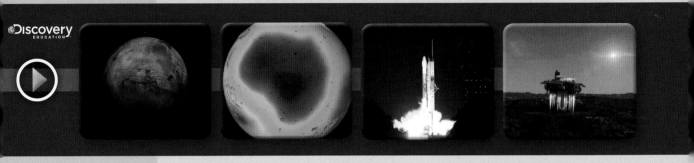

PREPARING TO WATCH

USING VISUALS TO PREDICT CONTENT

1 You are going to watch a video about space and astronomy. Work in pairs. Choose the correct definition of astronomy (a or b).

a the study of things in space, e.g. stars
b the study of space travel, e.g. space rockets

2 Work in pairs. Look at the picture. Discuss why you think there are lines in the rock.

UNDERSTANDING KEY VOCABULARY

3 Divide the words in the box into three groups: a equipment, b places and c people.

> solar system   astronaut   Mars
> telescope   planets   scientist
> astronomer   spacecraft   spacesuit

The surface of the planet Mars

4 Write the words from the table in the gaps to complete the sentences.

1 When Lee was a child he loved dressing as an _____ .
2 He used to put on a _____ and pretend that he was on the moon.
3 His father was a _____ and helped Lee with his science and maths homework.
4 When he was older Lee studied astronomy and became an _____ .
5 He learnt a lot about the _____ that the Earth is in.
6 He was very interested in different _____ such as Venus and _____ .
7 He used a _____ to look at the stars and planets.
8 One day he would like to go on a _____ and see some planets close up.

5 Work in pairs. Take turns to ask and answer the questions.

 1 Did you ever want to be an astronaut?
 2 Do you like astronomy?
 3 What do you know about planets like Mars?

WHILE WATCHING

6 ▶ Watch the video. Number the events (a–e) in the order that they happened.

 a The Odyssey took photos of Mars and found that there could be ice there.   ____
 b Now Curiosity Rover is exploring Mars.   ____
 c Phoenix Mars Lander arrived on Mars to study the history of water on the planet.   ____
 d A spacecraft took the first photograph of Mars in 1964.   ____
 e Phoenix Mars Lander found ice about one metre under the ground.   ____

6 ▶ Watch again. Why are the following dates important?

 1 2000   **2** 2002   **3** 2007   **4** 2008   **5** 2012

DISCUSSION

7 Work in pairs and answer the questions.

 1 Why is finding water on Mars so important?
 2 Do you think other planets have water? Why / Why not?
 3 Is water easy to find in your country? Why / Why not?

8 Match the sentences (1–3) to the definitions of the words in italics (a–c).

 1 *Fresh water* is important for life.
 2 Poor countries don't always have enough *running water* to drink and wash with.
 3 They travelled *by water*.

 a to go on a boat / ship
 b water without salt which you can drink
 c clean water sent to houses

9 Work in pairs and answer the questions.

 1 Is there a fresh water river or lake near your home?
 2 When was the last time you went somewhere by water?
 3 We use running water to wash, clean things and drink. If you had no running water for a day, what would you miss most?

LISTENING 1

PRONUNCIATION FOR LISTENING

1 🔊 **10.1** Listen to the sentences below. Underline two words in each sentence which sound the same.

1 When the sun is out, I make sure my son uses cream so he isn't burnt.
2 Have you read the information about the red planet?
3 We are having a picnic whether it is hot or not. It has been good weather recently so we are hoping it will be nice.
4 She ate her dinner before she went out at eight o'clock.
5 There are two doctors in the family and their daughter is also studying medicine.
6 Our visitor was in the house for an hour.

2 Work in pairs. Take turns to say the pairs of words (a and b) out loud. What do you notice about the spelling and the sound of the words?

1 a weather /weðə/   b whether /weðə/
2 a our /aʊə/   b hour /aʊə/
3 a sun /sʌn/   b son /sʌn/
4 a read /red/   b red /red/
5 a there /ðeə/   b their /ðeə/
6 a sent /sent/   b scent /sent/
7 a ate /eɪt/   b eight /eɪt/
8 a mined /maɪnd/   b mind /maɪnd/
9 a for /fɔː/   b four /fɔː/
10 a to /tuː/   b two /tuː/

3 🔊 **10.2** Listen to six sentences which have some of the words in Exercise 2. Write down each sentence as you listen.

PREPARING TO LISTEN

UNDERSTANDING KEY VOCABULARY

4 You're going to listen to a radio programme about space travel. Work in pairs. Read the questions and discuss the meaning of the words in bold.

1 Which **planets** can you name? What do you know about them?
2 What do we usually use **diamonds** for?
3 When talking about people does a **couple** mean friends or husband and wife?
4 Is a **project** something that is carefully planned or done quickly without plans?
5 Do people **explore** somewhere they already know or somewhere new?

5 Work in pairs. Take turns to ask and answer the questions in Exercise 4.

UNL◯CK LISTENING AND SPEAKING SKILLS 2

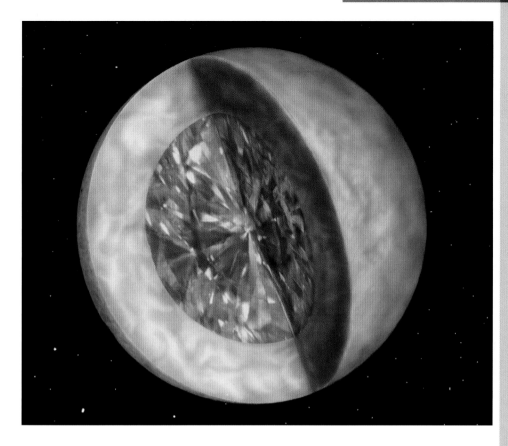

WHILE LISTENING

USING CONTEXT TO
GUESS WORDS

6 🔊 10.3 Listen to the first part of the radio programme. Write one word in each gap to complete the sentences.

1 We'll think about the planets people haven't visited yet and _____ we are likely to tour some of them in the future.

2 Let's begin inside _____ own solar system.

3 If someone asked you the name of a famous planet you would probably say Venus, Mars, Neptune or even the _____ .

4 Mars is known as the _____ Planet because of its colour.

5 There are now plans _____ send _____ people to visit it.

6 An organization called Inspiration Mars hopes to send the carefully selected people on the trip to Mars in the next _____ years.

Recognizing words with easily confused sounds

Some words sound the same or very similar. If the words sound the same you have to guess from the context which word is correct.

7 Read the sentences (1–6) in Exercise 6 again and check the spelling of the words you wrote.

8 🔊 **10.4** Listen to the second part of the listening. Decide if the following sentences are true or false.

    1 Inspiration Mars don't want a couple as they won't help each other on the journey.

    2 It is dangerous but a lot of people still want to go to Mars.

    3 The diamond planet is called 'Lucy'.

    4 Diamond planets are found in our solar system.

    5 Lucy is not as heavy as Earth.

    6 It turns so fast that one year passes in 24 hours.

9 🔊 **10.4** Listen to the second part of the listening again. Write down one more piece of information about the organization Inspiration Mars and one about the planet Lucy.

DISCUSSION

10 Work in pairs. Follow the instructions.

    1 Imagine you have found a new planet. Give it a name.

    2 Make a list of things you would like to find on the planet so it is a good place to live.

       • a warm temperature

       • not too hot or cold

11 Find another pair and share your ideas. Which of the planets do you like the best?

◉ LANGUAGE DEVELOPMENT

TRAVEL VERBS AND NOUNS WITH SIMILAR MEANINGS

UNLOCK ONLINE

1 Complete the gaps (1–6) in the table on page 183 with the words in italics in the box below. You will need one word more than once. Then check your answers with the glossary on page 208.

---

1 … we are looking at space *travel* and the journeys that people hope to make.

2 An organization called Inspiration Mars is planning to send a husband and wife on the *voyage*.

3 … the couple will be able to help each other when they go on the *journey* which will take 501 days.

4 … it will *travel* around the planet to get information.

5 Inspiration Mars hope the *trip* will be possible in the next four years.

A word	B definition
1 _____	**verb** to move from one place to another; to go on a journey to visit places **noun** used generally to describe the activity of moving from one place to another, often used after another noun e.g. *air* 2 _____ *train* 3 _____
4 _____	**noun** often found with *go on a*, *make a*; collocates with *long*, *train*, *bus*, *return*; usually describes travel over a long distance
5 _____	**noun** often found with *take a*, *make a* or *go on a*; collocates with *business* and *shopping*; usually means a journey with a special reason
6 _____	**noun** a journey by sea or in space but usually from one place to another i.e. A➜B
7 flight	**noun** a journey by air
8 cruise	**noun** travel by sea; usually this means visiting many places, not just one for pleasure i.e. A➜B➜C➜D➜A

2 Write a word from the table in the gaps to complete the sentences. In some cases more than one answer is possible.

1 One day I would like to go on a _____ by train across China.
2 How often do you _____ to other countries?
3 We went on a three week _____ in the South Pacific and visited a lot of the islands.
4 The Airbus 350 _____ to Saigon leaves from Gate 23.
5 My brother is on a business _____ in Tokyo.
6 The _____ of the space shuttle from the Earth to the moon took three and a half days.
7 I spent far too much money on my shopping _____ .
8 In the past, before planes, a _____ from Europe to the USA took 43 days and people on the ship were often ill.

3 Work in pairs. Take turns to tell your partner the answers to the questions.

1 What is your favourite journey?
2 How do you like to travel when you go on holiday?
3 Would you ever like to go on a cruise?
4 When was the last time you took a flight or went on a trip?

CONDITIONALS

4 Match the sentence halves.

1 If the planet Lucy were mined,
2 If they find a married couple for the space voyage,

a they believe the couple can help each other.
b there would be more diamonds than on Earth.

5 Work in pairs. Match the conditional sentences in Exercise 4 to the functions (i–iii).

i describes something which is possible
ii describes something which is imaginary / hypothetical

6 Write the sentences from Exercise 4 in the table.

condition clause	result clause
if + present tense	*will / can*
if + past tense	*would / could*

7 Match the situations (1–6) to the functions (i–ii) in Exercise 5 and choose the correct verb form.

1 If I *meet / met* my friend later, we *will / would* go to the cinema.
2 If I *meet / met* the president or leader of my country I *won't / wouldn't* know what to say.
3 If I *speak / spoke* perfect English, I *will / would* be very proud.
4 If I *lose / lost* my phone, I *will / would* have to buy a new one.
5 If the weather *is / was* good tomorrow, I *will / would* go out.
6 You *can / could* travel into space if you *have / had* enough money.

8 Work in pairs. Discuss whether the sentences in Exercise 7 are true for you.

LISTENING 2

PREPARING TO LISTEN

1 Write letters in the gaps to complete the words in the table. Then check your answers with the glossary on page 208.

UNDERSTANDING
KEY VOCABULARY

verb	person	noun
1 e _ _ _ _ e	2 e _ _ _ _ _ er	exploration
3 r _ _ _ _ _ ch	researcher	4 r _ _ _ _ _ ch
work	5 w _ _ k _ _	6 _ _ _ k
travel	7 _ _ _ v _ ll _ _	travel
present	8 p _ _ _ _ _ _ er	9 p _ _ _ _ _ _ _ tion
think	10 th _ _ _ _ r	thought

PRONUNCIATION FOR LISTENING

2 Work in pairs. Say the words in bold in Exercise 1 out loud. Does the *t* in both words sound different or the same?

3 Work in pairs. Say the words out loud.

/t/	/ɵ/
1 tree	2 three
3 tank	4 thank
5 bat	6 bath
7 true	8 through

4 🔊 10.5 Listen, check and repeat.

5 Work in pairs and look at the phrases from the listening. Underline the /t/ and /ɵ/ sounds then say the phrases aloud.

> 1 We'll think about the type…
> 2 and whether it is worth it.

WHILE LISTENING

6 You are going to listen to a discussion about the International Space Station. Work in pairs. Look at the photograph and answer the questions.

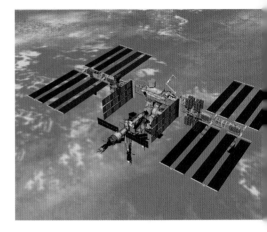

1 Have you seen photographs of the International Space Station before?
2 What do you think it is used for?

7 ◀)) 10.6 Listen to part one of the talk introducing the discussion. Write words in the gaps to complete sentences from the introduction.

1 We'll begin today's discussion with a look at space _____ .
2 We'll think about what type of _____ the space station does and whether the _____ we spend is worth it. We will then look at the _____ of the station.

8 You are going to listen to part two of the discussion. What do you think the function of the discussion will be? Choose the most probable option. (1–3)

1 to describe what the Space Station looks like
2 to evaluate the Space Station and its good and bad points
3 to invent a new Space Station which can do different things

9 Work in pairs. Predict the topics (1–6) that will be included in the discussion.

1 time taken to travel to the Space Station
2 the type of work done on the Space Station
3 routines of living there
4 money spent on the project
5 the number of astronauts working there
6 types of space shuttle to travel there

10 ◀)) 10.7 Listen to the part two of the discussion between Chen, Raj and Dorota. Check your answers to Exercises 8 and 9.

11 ◀)) 10.7 Listen again. Match the people (1–3) with their opinion about the space station (a–c).

1 Dorota Loy   a thinks it is important for learning about space travel
2 Professor Chen b thinks it is important but has to help the Earth
3 Raj Padow   c thinks it can help with space travel and the Earth

DISCUSSION

12 Work in small groups. Look at the picture below and discuss the questions.

    1 Do you think this will happen in the future?
    2 What are the benefits for people?
    3 Are there any disadvantages?
    4 Would you like to live there? Why / Why not?
    5 If you lived there, what would you do in your free time?

Possible future settlement on the moon

CRITICAL THINKING

At the end of this unit you are going to do the speaking task below.

Plan a conference about space exploration. Discuss and find solutions to any possible problems.

1 Work in pairs. You are going to start an astronomy club. Discuss the kinds of problems that can happen when you are planning to start a new club or event. Use the ideas (1–4) below to help you.

    1 times

    _____
    _____

    2 place

    _____
    _____

    3 people coming regularly

    _____
    _____

APPLY

Question charts

Question charts are useful for examining the key points of an issue or event. Use the chart to plan the times, people, topics, places, and methods of your project.

2 Write the points (1–5) in the chart .

  1 lunchtimes: a lot of people around / would keep everyone busy
  2 choose a weekly topic and everyone brings in ideas each week
  3 open to anyone who is interested in astronomy
  4 in the corner of the café
  5 a club to help us discuss new discoveries or topics on astronomy

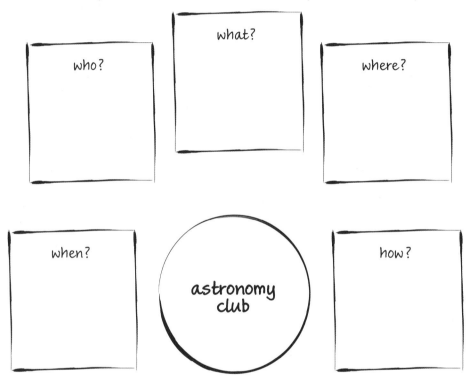

3 Work in small groups. Discuss the questions about problem solving.

  1 What is the best way to think of different ideas? Give reasons for your thoughts. Look back at the different charts in the units of the book to help you.
  2 Is it important to support your ideas with more information? Why / Why not?

SPEAKING

PREPARATION FOR SPEAKING

1 What can you do when someone else is talking to show that you are interested or that you are bored?

2 Work in pairs. Take it in turns to talk about the topics below. When you are listening, show interest or show that you are bored. Your partner should guess if you are interested or not.

1 my favourite place to visit at the weekend

2 a person I admire

3 the last journey I made

4 my best friend

5 my favourite meal

6 an interesting job

3 We often use fixed phrases to invite others to speak, interrupt or continue speaking when someone stopped us. Write the phrases (a–j) in the correct column of the table below.

a What is your opinion?
b Can I finish?
c I'd like to finish my point.
d Can I just cut in there?
e Sorry but I have to interrupt you and say...
f You haven't said much. What do you think?
g Why don't you start us off...
h Sorry but can I just say...
i Would anybody like to say anything else about...?
j Let me just finish what I was saying.

inviting someone else to speak	interrupting	continuing to speak
Let's get your thoughts on this. _____ _____ _____ _____ _____ _____ _____	Can I just say something here? _____ _____ _____ _____ _____	Can I finish my point? Please allow me to finish. _____ _____ _____ _____ _____

4 Write the phrases from the table in Exercise 3 in the gaps to complete the conversation between five people. More than one answer is possible for some gaps.

Halil   We are discussing the best way to travel when going on holiday. ⁽¹⁾ _____ Ramona?

Ramona   For me it is definitely the train. You can relax and watch the world go by as you travel-

Shin   ⁽²⁾_____ . Doesn't that depend on the train? In many cities you can't sit down because they are too crowded and-

Ramona   ⁽³⁾_____ . You can relax and watch the world go by but this has to be in a city where the trains are not too busy. If you are on a commuter train it wouldn't be very nice.

Halil   ⁽⁴⁾_____ trains?

Lisa   No but I'd like to talk about bikes. They are the most economical way to travel.

Ramona   I agree. It is another good way to travel.

Halil   And Francoise, ⁽⁵⁾_____ . What do you think? ⁽⁶⁾ _____ .

Francoise   Sorry! I wasn't listening!

5 Work in small groups and read the dialogue out loud.

6 Divide the phrases into those we use to start a discussion and those we use to finish a discussion. Write *S* (start) or *F* (finish).

1 Let me begin by asking …   _____

2 Let me finish this off by saying …   _____

3 We'll begin today's discussion with a look at …   _____

4 Would you like to start us off?   _____

5 So to conclude …   _____

6 Finally …   _____

7 Work in groups of three and discuss the topics in Exercise 2 on page 189. Start and finish discussing the topics with the phrases from Exercise 6.

SPEAKING TASK

> Plan a conference about space exploration. Discuss and find solutions to any possible problems.

1 Work in pairs. Discuss what you think happens at a conference.

2 Work in small groups. You have to organize a conference. Read the details of your task below. Think of any problems that could possibly happen at a conference.

The conference will be about space exploration. It will look at research into ways of developing our abilities in space (e.g. starting a space camp on the moon).
You need to:
• discuss and decide what your conference will be about
• decide when you would run it e.g. winter/ summer
• identify who you would invite and how e.g. advertising/ private invitations
• explain where the conference will be and what the venue is like
• provide a timetable for the conference
• outline the social events and other activities you will include
• Finally, you will present your ideas for organizing the conference to your colleagues.

3 Work in small groups and plan your conference. Follow the steps below.

• Create a question chart with your ideas.
• Use the chart from Exercise 2 page 188 as an example to help you.
• Make sure that you discuss possible problems and solutions.
• Use the language in the Preparation for speaking on page 189 in your discussion.

4 You are going to present your plan to another group. Number the information in the order that you will present it.

  a Explain who will be invited. _____
  b Describe what the conference is about. _____
  c Talk about extra events e.g. social activities. _____
  d Give details of the time and timetable / venue. _____

5 Work with another group. Take turns to present your ideas and to listen. Make notes on the other group's ideas and any problems you think of with their plan.

6 In the same group, decide which ideas are best for each part of the conference.

7 Compare your final plan with other groups. Which is the best?

TASK CHECKLIST	✔
Did you use a question chart to discuss ideas?	
Did you sound interested when someone is speaking?	
Did you discuss possible problems and solutions?	
Did you use conditionals accurately?	
Do you know phrases for turn-taking and for starting and finishing a discussion?	

OBJECTIVES REVIEW

I can ...

watch and understand a video about space.

very well   not very well

listen for easily confused words.

very well   not very well

use a question chart to think of ideas.

very well   not very well

take turns in discussions and show I am interested.

very well   not very well

solve problems.

very well   not very well

WORDLIST

UNIT VOCABULARY	
astronomy (n)	presentation (n)
by / on water (phr)	presenter (n)
conference (n)	project (n)
couple (n)	research (v) (n)
cruise (n)	researcher (n)
diamond (n)	space (n)
exploration (n)	travel (v) (n)
explore (v)	traveller (n)
explorer (n)	trip (n)
flight (n)	voyage (n)
fly (v)	whether (prep)
journey (n)	work (v)
present (v)	worker (n)

PAIRWORK ACTIVITIES

STUDENT A

UNIT 1

Sentenil de Las Bodegas, Spain

1 Look at the photograph. Write the words in the box in the correct row of the table.

> castle built: 12th century   first people in caves, then built into mountain side
> houses: possibly dark?   in Spain   located 157 miles northeast of Cadiz
> people lived there: Roman times   unusual   nice building

A plan for talk	B information in each part of talk
introduction	
general facts / history	
opinion: advantages	
opinion: disadvantages	
summary	

2 Work in pairs. Present the information in the table to your partner.

UNIT 7

You are a famous football star. What do you think about people in sport earning a lot of money? Why? Use the ideas rakes you created on page 137 to help you.

UNIT 8

1 Tell student B your problems. Use the ideas below. Then listen to student B's advice.

   1 Everyone is late for meetings and wastes my time.
   2 When I speak English in the meeting I get too nervous to speak.
   3 People in class chat when I am trying to learn.
   4 You can't use the computer very well.

2 Listen to student B's problems. Give him / her some advice.

UNIT 9

Describe the vacuum cleaner to Student B. Then listen to Student B and label the photograph of the shopping trolley.

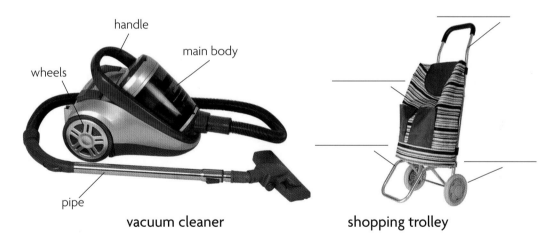

vacuum cleaner   **shopping trolley**

UNIT 1

Hadhramaut, Yemen

1 Look at the photograph. Write the words in the box in the correct row of the table.

in Shibam, centre of Yemen   mud houses: built 16th century
dangerous   unusual   some of the mud houses: 30 metres high
old   in the desert of Ramlat al sab'atayn   dangerous in rain
rebuilt many times over last hundred years   very interesting place to live

A plan for talk	B information in each part of talk
introduction	
general facts / history	
opinion: advantages	
opinion: disadvantages	
summary	

2 Work in pairs. Present the information in the table to your partner.

UNIT 5

1 Look at the pictures showing the process of sending an instant message and check you understand the process.

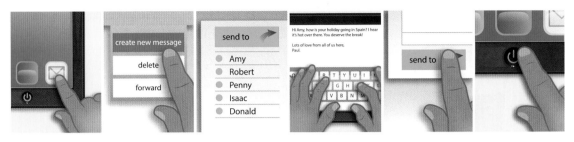

2 Check you understand the meaning of the words in the box.

> **nouns** message   address book   list   button   switch off   recipients
> **verbs**   select   send   type   choose   press
> **sequencing words**   firstly   next   finally

3 Use the flow chart below to prepare your instructions.

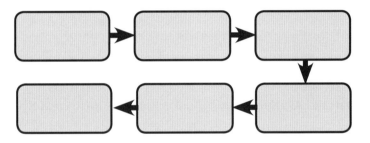

UNIT 7

You are a charity worker. Your charity helps poor people get food and medicine. What do you think about the money spent on sports men and women? Why? Use the ideas rakes you created on page 137 to help you.

UNIT 8

1 Listen to student A's problems. Give him / her some advice.

2 Tell student A your problems. Use the ideas below. Then listen to student A's advice.

1 People leave the room very untidy after the lesson and you have to tidy it.
2 You keep forgetting meetings and appointments.
3 Your boss/teacher forgets to check your work.
4 You find it difficult to do presentations as you get too nervous.

UNIT 9

Describe the shopping trolley to Student A. Then listen and label the photograph of the vacuum cleaner.

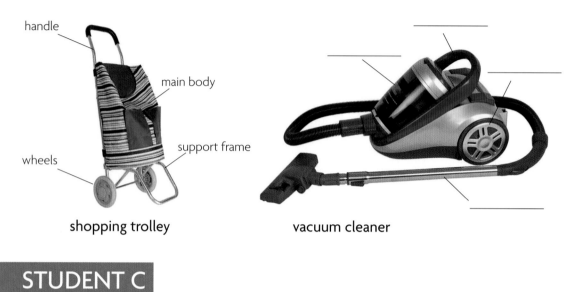

handle

main body

support frame

wheels

shopping trolley

vacuum cleaner

STUDENT C

UNIT 7

You are a journalist and you write about sports for the newspaper. What do you think about the money spent on sports men and women? Why? Use the idea rakes you created on page 137 to help you.

STUDENT D

UNIT 7

You are the moderator of the panel discussion. You are going to ask the panel to give their ideas. You will need to ask each person their idea before a general discussion.

GLOSSARY

Vocabulary	Pronunciation	Part of speech	Definition
UNIT 1			
advantage	/əd'vɑːntɪdʒ/	(n)	something good about a situation that helps you
ancient	/'eɪntʃənt/	(adj)	from a long time ago
beautiful	/'bjuːtɪfəl/	(adj)	very attractive
believe	/bɪ'liːv/	(v)	to think that something is true, or that what someone says is true
bridge	/brɪdʒ/	(n)	a structure that is built over a river, road, railway, etc. to allow people and vehicles to cross from one side to the other
bus stop	/bʌs stɒp/	(n)	a place where a bus stops to allow passengers to get on and off
castle	/'kɑːsəl/	(n)	a large strong building with towers and high walls that was built in the past to protect the people inside from being attacked
cave	/'keɪv/	(n)	a large hole in the side of a mountain or underground
clear	/klɪə/	(adj)	easy to understand, hear, read or see
coffee shop	/'kɒfi ʃɒp/	(n)	a place where you can buy hot drinks, cakes and small meals
complex	/'kɒmpleks/	(adj)	detailed and difficult to understand
complicated	/'kɒmplɪkeɪtɪd/	(adj)	difficult to understand
cottage	/'kɒtɪdʒ/	(n)	a small house, usually in the countryside
dangerous	/'deɪndʒərəs/	(adj)	If someone or something is dangerous, they could harm you.
desert	/'dezət/	(n)	a large, hot, dry area of land with very few plants
fact	/fækt/	(n)	something that you know is true, exists, or has happened
feel	/fiːl/	(v)	to think something or have an opinion
field	/fiːld/	(n)	an area of land used for growing crops or keeping animals
finally	/'faɪnəli/	(adv)	used especially at the beginning of a sentence to introduce the last point or idea
firstly	/'fɜːstli/	(adv)	used to refer to the first thing in a list
forest	/'fɒrɪst/	(n)	a large area of trees growing closely together
industrial	/ɪn'dʌstriəl//	(adj)	connected to industry
journey	/'dʒɜːni/	(n)	when you travel from one place to another
lake	/leɪk/	(n)	a large area of water which has land all around it
located	/ləʊ'keɪtɪd/	(v)	to be in a particular place
long	/lɒŋ/	(adj)	having a large distance from one end to the other
lovely	/'lʌvli/	(adj)	pleasant or enjoyable
method	/'meθəd/	(n)	a way of doing something, often one that involves a system or plan
mountain	/'maʊntɪn/	(n)	a raised part of the Earth's surface, much larger than a hill, the top of which might be covered in snow
mushroom-shaped	/'mʌʃrʊm ʃeɪpt/	(adj)	having the shape of a mushroom
obviously	/'ɒbviəsli/	(adv)	in a way that is easy to understand or see
opinion	/ə'pɪnjən/	(n)	a thought or belief about something or someone
personally	/'pɜːsənəli/	(adv)	used when you give your opinion
process	/prəʊ'ses/	(v)	to understand information
recognize	/'rekəgnaɪz/	(v)	to know someone or something because you have seen, heard, or experienced them before
river	/'rɪvə/	(n)	a long, natural area of water that flows across the land and into a sea, lake, or another river
rock	/rɒk/	(n)	the hard, natural substance which forms part of the Earth's surface, or an area of this substance sticking out of the sea or ground
route	/ruːt/	(n)	the roads or paths you follow to get from one place to another place

Vocabulary	Pronunciation	Part of speech	Definition
satnav	/ˈsætnæv/	(n)	abbreviation for satellite navigation: a system of computers and satellite equipment used in cars and other places to tell a user where they are or where something is
strange	/streɪndʒ/	(adj)	If something is strange, it is surprising because it is unusual or unexpected.
street	/striːt/	(n)	a road in a town or city that has houses or other buildings
think	/θɪŋk/	(v)	to have an opinion about something or someone
tour	/tʊr/	(n)	a visit to and around a place, area, or country
tourist information office	/ˈtʊrɪst ˌɪnfəˈmeɪʃən ˈɒfɪs/	(n)	an office that supplies information to people who are visiting an area for pleasure or interest
traffic lights	/ˈtræfɪklaɪts/	(n)	red, green, and yellow lights that are used to stop and start traffic
trip	/trɪp/	(n)	a journey in which you visit a place for a short time and come back again
unusual	/ʌnˈjuːʒəl/	(adj)	different and not ordinary, often in a way that is interesting or exciting
way	/weɪ/	(n)	the route you take to get from one place to another
wildlife	/ˈwaɪldlaɪf/	(n)	animals and plants that grow independently of people, usually in natural conditions
UNIT 2			
activity	/ækˈtɪvəti/	(n)	something that is done for enjoyment, especially an organized event
band	/bænd/	(n)	a group of musicians who play modern music together
bride	/braɪd/	(n)	a woman who is getting married
camel	/ˈkæməl/	(n)	a large animal that lives in the desert and has one or two raised parts on its back
celebration	/ˌseləˈbreɪʃən/	(n)	a special social event, such as a party, when you celebrate something, or the act of celebrating something
culture	/ˈkʌltʃə/	(n)	the way of life, especially the habits, traditions and beliefs, of a particular group of people at a particular time
decoration	/ˌdekəˈreɪʃən/	(n)	a thing used to make something more attractive
dish	/dɪʃ/	(n)	food prepared in a particular way as part of a meal
dried fruit	/draɪd fruːt/	(n)	fruit that has been dried to stop it from decaying
entertainment	/entəˈteɪnmənt/	(n)	shows, films, television, or other performances or activities that entertain people, or a performance of this type
festival	/ˈfestɪvəl/	(n)	a special day or period when people celebrate something
groom	/gruːm/	(n)	a man who is getting married
have a celebration / a party	/hæv ə ˈpɑːti/	(phr)	to have a social event where a group of people meet to talk, eat, drink, dance, etc., often in order to celebrate a special occasion
have fun / a nice time	/hæv ˈfʌn/	(phr)	to enjoy yourself
have a problem	/hæv ə ˈprɒbləm/	(phr)	when you are in a situation that needs help
interesting	/ˈɪntrəstɪŋ/	(adj)	Someone or something that is interesting keeps your attention because they are unusual, exciting, or have a lot of ideas.
interested in	/ˈɪntrəstɪd ɪn/	(v)	give your attention to something and discover more about it
layer	/ˈleɪə/	(n)	an amount of a substance covering a surface
lecture	/ˈlektʃə/	(n)	a formal talk on a serious or specialist subject given to a group of people, especially students
noodle	/ˈnuːdəl/	(n)	thin pieces of pasta
take advice	/teɪk ədˈvaɪs/	(phr)	to follow an opinion that someone gives you
take a test	/teɪk ə ˈtest/	(phr)	a set of questions used to find out how much someone knows
take care (of)	/teɪk ˈkeər/	(phr)	to be careful; to be in charge of someone or something

Vocabulary	Pronunciation	Part of speech	Definition
take your time	/teɪk jɔː ˈtaɪm/	(phr)	to use as much time as is required
traditional	/trəˈdɪʃənəl/	(adj)	following the customs or ways of behaving that have continued in a group of people or society for a long time

UNIT 3

Vocabulary	Pronunciation	Part of speech	Definition
agree	/əˈgriː/	(v)	to have the same opinion
apologize	/əˈpɒlədʒaɪz/	(v)	to tell someone that you are sorry for having done something that has caused them problems or unhappiness
Art	/ɑːt/	(n)	making or study of paintings, drawings, etc. or the objects created
begin	/ˈbəgɪn /	(v)	to start to happen
Biology	/baɪˈɒlədʒi/	(n)	the scientific study of living things
blended learning	/blendɪd lɜːnɪŋ/	(n)	using technology and traditional classroom learning together
chairperson	/ˈtʃeəpɜːsən/	(n)	someone who controls a meeting, company, or other organization
Chemistry	/ˈkemɪstri/	(n)	the scientific study of substances and the different ways in which they react or combine with other substances
classroom	/ˈklɑːsrʊm/	(n)	a room in a school or college where groups of students are taught
computer room	/kəmˈpjuːtə ruːm/	(n)	a room where there are several computers available to use
concentrate	/ˈkɒntsəntreɪt/	(v)	to direct your attention or your efforts towards a particular activity, subject, or problem
cook	/kʊk/	(v)	to prepare food and usually heat it
corridor	/ˈkɒrɪdɔː/	(n)	a long passage in a building or train
enjoy	/ɪnˈdʒɔɪ /	(v)	to get pleasure from something
first-floor	/ˈfɜːst flɔː/	(n)	the level of a building that is one level above the street
French	/frentʃ/	(adj)	coming from or relating to France
Geography	/dʒiˈɒgrəfi/	(n)	the study of the surface of the Earth and all regions of the world
ground floor	/graʊnd flɔː/	(n)	the floor of a building that is at the same level as the ground outside
History	/ˈhɪstəri/	(n)	the study of events in the past
laboratory	/ləˈbɒrətəri/	(n)	a room used for scientific work
learn	/lɜːn/	(v)	to get knowledge or skill in a new subject or activity
lecturer	/ˈlektʃərə/	(n)	someone who teaches at a university or college
library	/ˈlaɪbrəri/	(n)	a room or building that contains a collection of books and other written material that you can read or borrow
Maths	/mæθs/	(n)	the study of numbers, shapes and space using reason and usually a special system of symbols and rules for organizing them
mind	/maɪnd/	(v)	to be annoyed or worried by something
office	/ˈɒfɪs/	(n)	a room or building where people work
online learning	/ɒnˈlaɪn lɜːnɪŋ/	(n)	learning a subject via technology
Physics	/ˈfɪzɪks/	(n)	the scientific study of matter and energy and the effect that they have on each other
plan	/plæn/	(v)	to intend to do something or that an event or result should happen
revise	/rɪˈvaɪz/	(v)	to study a subject before you take a test
sports field	/spɔːts ˈfiːld/	(n)	a field where people play sports
stair	/steə/	(n)	one of the steps in a set of steps
start	/stɑːt/	(v)	to begin
study	/ˈstʌdi/	(v)	to learn about a subject, especially on an educational course or by reading books
teach	/tiːtʃ/	(v)	to give lessons in a particular subject at a school, university, etc.
teacher	/ˈtiːtʃə/	(n)	someone whose job is to teach in a school or college
team leader	/tiːm ˈliːdə/	(n)	someone who manages a team of people
want	/wɒnt /	(v)	to wish for a particular thing or plan of action

Vocabulary	Pronunciation	Part of speech	Definition
UNIT 4			
advertise	/ˈædvətaɪz/	(v)	to tell people about a product or service in newspapers, on television, on the Internet, etc.
also	/ˈɔːlsəʊ/	(adv)	in addition
app	/æp/	(n)	abbreviation for application: a computer program that is designed for a particular purpose
as	/æz/	(conj)	because
as well as	/æz wel æz/	(adv)	and / also
battery	/ˈbætəri/	(n)	a device that produces electricity to provide power for mobile phones, laptop computers, radios, cars, etc.
because of	/bɪˈkɒz ɒv/	(prep)	as a result of
but	/bʌt/	(conj)	used to introduce an added statement, usually something that is different from what you have said before
charger	/ˈtʃɑːdʒə/	(n)	a device that is used to recharge a battery (=fill it with electricity), for example in a mobile phone
difficult	/ˈdɪfɪkəlt/	(adj)	when something is not easy to do or understand
disabled	/dɪˈseɪbəld/	(adj)	having an illness, injury or condition that makes it difficult to do the things that most people do
download	/daʊnˈləʊd/	(v)	to copy computer programs, music or other information electronically, especially from the Internet or a larger computer
due to	/dʒuː tuː/	(prep)	because of
file	/faɪl/	(n)	a collection of information such as text, pictures or computer programs stored together electronically with a single name
go online	/gəʊ ɒnˈlaɪn/	(phr)	use the internet
however	/haʊˈevə/	(adv)	used when you are about to say something which contrasts with what you have just said
keyboard	/ˈkiːbɔːd/	(n)	a set of keys that you press to use a computer
location	/ləʊˈkeɪʃən/	(n)	a place or position
log on	/lɒg ɒn/	(v)	to connect to a computer or a website
memory	/ˈmeməri/	(n)	your ability to remember
mouse	/maʊs/	(n)	a small piece of equipment connected to a computer that you move with your hand to control what the computer does
on the other hand	/ɒn ðiː ˈʌðə hænd/	(phr)	used when you are about to say something which contrasts with what you have just said
scientist	/ˈsaɪəntɪst/	(n)	someone who studies science or works in science
shut down	/ˈʃʌtdaʊn/	(v)	to turn off a computer
stupid	/ˈstjuːpɪd/	(adj)	silly or not intelligent
suit	/suːt/	(n)	an outfit that is made from the same material
surf	/sɜːf/	(v)	to look at information on the Internet by moving from one page to another using electronic links
switch on / off	/swɪtʃ ɒn / ɒf/	(v)	turn the power on/off
text	/tekst/	(v)	to send someone a text message
thanks to	/θæŋks tuː/	(phr)	because of
the cloud	/klaʊd/	(n)	a computer network where files and programs can be stored, especially the internet
water pollution	/ˈwɔːtə pəˈluːʃən/	(n)	damage caused to water by harmful substances or waste
whereas	/hweəˈræz/	(conj)	compared with the fact that
wi-fi	/ˈwaɪfaɪ/	(n)	a system for connecting electronic equipment such as computers and electronic organizers to the Internet without using wires

Vocabulary	Pronunciation	Part of speech	Definition
UNIT 5			
after that	/ˈɑːftə ðæt/	(phr)	said before the next thing in a list
ask	/ɑːsk/	(v)	to say a question to someone which you want them to answer
at the end	/ət ðiː end/	(phr)	said to introduce the last bit of a list or instructions
blind	/blaɪnd/	(adj)	not able to see
button	/ˈbʌt.ən/	(n)	a switch that you press to control a piece of equipment
chin	/tʃɪn/	(n)	the bottom part of a person's face, below their mouth
cursor	/ˈkɜːsə/	(n)	a symbol on a computer screen which shows the place where you are working
deaf	/def/	(adj)	unable to hear, either completely or partly
finger	/ˈfɪŋɡə/	(n)	one of the long thin separate parts of the hand, including your thumb
finally	/ˈfaɪnəli/	(adv)	used especially at the beginning of a sentence to introduce the last point or idea
lid	/lɪd/	(n)	a cover on a container, which can be lifted up or removed
lip	/lɪp/	(n)	one of the two soft edges of the mouth
mouth	/maʊθ/	(n)	the part of the face that is used for eating and speaking
nationality	/næʃənˈæləti/	(n)	If you have American/British/Swiss, etc. nationality, you are legally a member of that country.
palm	/pɑːm/	(n)	the inside surface of your hand
pat	/pæt/	(v)	to touch a person or animal with a flat hand in a gentle, friendly way
photocopier	/ˈfəʊtəʊkɒpiə/	(n)	a machine which makes copies of papers
pick up	/ˈpɪkʌp/	(v)	to learn new skill or language through practising rather than being taught it
press	/pres/	(v)	to push something firmly
say	/seɪ/	(v)	to speak words
select	/sɪˈlekt/	(v)	to choose someone or something from a group
send	/send/	(v)	to arrange for something to go somewhere, especially by post
smell	/smel/	(v)	to notice something by using your nose
speak	/spiːk/	(v)	to say something using your voice
straighten	/ˈstreɪtən/	(v)	to become straight or to make something straight
tell	/tel/	(v)	to say something to someone, usually giving them information
thumb	/θʌm/	(n)	the short thick finger on the side of your hand which makes it possible to hold and pick things up easily
to finish	/tuː ˈfɪnɪʃ/	(phr)	used before saying the last thing in a list or presentation
to start with	/tuː stɑːt wɪð/	(phr)	used before saying the first thing in a list of things
wave	/weɪv/	(v)	to raise your hand and move it from side to side in order to attract someone's attention or to say goodbye
UNIT 6			
as a result	/æz ə rɪˈzʌlt/	(phr)	because of
burn	/bɜːn/	(v)	to damage or destroy by fire or extreme heat
calm	/kɑːm/	(adj)	relaxed and not worried, frightened, or excited
chilly	/ˈtʃɪli/	(adj)	unpleasantly cold
climate change	/ˈklaɪmət tʃeɪndʒ/	(n)	the way the Earth's weather is changing
cut down (sth)	/kʌt daʊn/	(v)	to make a tree or plant fall to the ground by cutting it near the bottom
damage	/ˈdæmɪdʒ/	(v)	to harm, break or spoil something
disease	/dɪˈziːz/	(n)	(an) illness caused by infection or by a failure of health rather than by an accident
disappear	/dɪsəˈpɪə/	(v)	to no longer exist
drinking water	/drɪŋkɪŋ ˈwɔːtə/	(n)	water that is safe for people to drink

Vocabulary	Pronunciation	Part of speech	Definition
drought	/draʊt/	(n)	a long period when there is not enough rain or water
dull	/dʌl/	(adj)	not bright
energetic	/enəˈdʒetɪk/	(adj)	having or involving a lot of energy
exciting	/ɪkˈsaɪtɪŋ/	(adj)	making you feel very happy and enthusiastic
factory	/ˈfæktəri/	(n)	a building or set of buildings where large amounts of goods are made using machines
flood	/flʌd/	(v)	If a place floods or is flooded, it becomes covered in water.
foggy weather	/ˈfɒgi ˈweðə/	(phr)	weather in which there is a lot of fog
forest	/ˈfɒrɪst/	(n)	a large area of trees growing closely together
fossil fuel	/ˈfɒsəl ˈfjuːəl/	(n)	a fuel such as coal or oil that is obtained from under the ground
frog	/frɒg/	(n)	a small, green animal with long back legs for jumping that lives in or near water
gas	/gæs/	(n)	a substance in a form like air that is used as a fuel for heating and cooking
global warming	/ˈgləʊbəl wɔːmɪŋ/	(n)	a gradual increase in world temperatures caused by polluting gases
humid	/ˈhjuːmɪd/	(adj)	humid air or weather is hot and slightly wet.
ice	/aɪs/	(n)	water that has frozen and become solid
interested	/ˈɪntrəstɪd/	(adj)	wanting to give your attention to something and discover more about it
melt	/melt/	(v)	to change from a solid into a liquid
prevent	/prɪˈvent/	(v)	to stop something from happening or someone from doing something
protect	/prəˈtekt/	(v)	to keep someone or something safe from something dangerous or bad
rainfall	/ˈreɪnfɔːl/	(n)	the amount of rain that falls in a particular place at a particular time
rainforest	/ˈreɪnfɒrɪst/	(n)	a forest in a tropical area which receives a lot of rain
sea levels	/siː ˈlevəlz/	(n)	the average height of the sea where it meets the land
smoke	/sməʊk/	(n)	the grey or black gas that is produced when something burns
so	/səʊ/	(conj)	used to say that something is the reason why something else happens
species	/ˈspiːʃiːz/	noun	a group of plants or animals which share similar characteristics
temperature	/ˈtemprətʃə/	(n)	how hot or cold something is
therefore	/ˈðeəfɔː/	(adv)	for that reason
trap heat	/træp hiːt/	(phr)	to keep heat in one place
wildlife	/ˈwaɪldlaɪf/	(n)	animals and plants that grow independently of people in their natural environment

UNIT 7

actually	/ˈæktʃuəli/	(adv)	used when you are emphasizing what is really true or what really happened
advantage	/ədˈvɑːntɪdʒ/	(n)	something good about a situation that helps you
already	/ɔːlˈredi/	(adv)	before now, or before a particular time in the past
benefit	/ˈbenɪfɪt/	(n)	something that helps you or gives you an advantage
best	/best/	(adj)	(superlative of good) better than any other
board	/bɔːd/	(n)	a flat piece of wood, cardboard, etc. for playing games on
boxing	/bɒksɪŋ/	(n)	a sport in which two competitors fight by hitting each other with their hands
chess	/tʃes/	(n)	a game that two people play by moving differently shaped pieces around a board of black and white squares
club	/klʌb/	(n)	one of a set of specially shaped wooden or metal sticks used for hitting a golf ball
compete	/kəmˈpiːt/	(v)	to take part in a race or competition

Vocabulary	Pronunciation	Part of speech	Definition
competition	/kɒmpəˈtɪʃən/	(n)	an organized event in which people try to win a prize by being the best, fastest, etc.
competitive	/kəmˈpetɪtɪv/	(adj)	wanting very much to win or be more successful than other people
competitor	/kəmˈpetɪtə/	(n)	a person, team or company that is competing against others
course	/kɔːs/	(n)	an area of land or water used for a sports event
court	/kɔːt/	(n)	an area drawn out on the ground which is used for playing sports such as tennis and basketball
cup	/kʌp/	(n)	a specially designed cup, usually with two handles and often made of silver, which is given as a prize in a sports competition, or a game or match in which the winner receives such a cup
definitely	/ˈdefɪnətli/	(adv)	without any doubt
disadvantage	/dɪsədˈvɑːntɪdʒ/	(n)	something which makes a situation more difficult, or makes you less likely to succeed
ever	/ˈevə/	(adv)	at any time
football	/ˈfʊtbɔːl/	(n)	a game in which two teams of players kick a round ball and try to score goals
game	/geɪm/	(n)	a particular competition, match or occasion when people play a game
glove	/glʌv/	(n)	a piece of clothing which covers your fingers and hand
goal	/gəʊl/	(n)	a point scored in sports such as soccer, when a player sends a ball or other object into a particular area, such as between two posts
golf	/gɒlf/	(n)	a game on grass where players try to hit a small ball into a series of holes, using a long, thin stick
helmet	/ˈhelmət/	(n)	a hard hat that protects your head
hit	/hɪt/	(v)	to touch someone or something quickly and with force using your hand or an object in your hand
ice skating	/ˈaɪsskeɪtɪŋ/	(n)	the activity or sport of moving across ice using ice skates
just	/dʒʌst/	(adv)	a very short time ago
kick	/kɪk/	(v)	to hit someone or something with the foot, or to move the feet and legs suddenly and violently
lose	/luːz/	(v)	to fail to succeed in a game, competition, etc.
obviously	/ˈɒbviəsli/	(adv)	in a way that is easy to understand or see
piece	/piːs/	(n)	a single object of a particular type
player	/pleɪə/	(n)	someone who takes part in a game or sport
prize	/praɪz/	(n)	something valuable that is given to someone who wins a competition or who has done good work
probably	/ˈprɒbəbli/	(adv)	used to mean that something is very likely
racquet	/ˈrækɪt/	(n)	an object used for hitting the ball in various sports, consisting of a net fixed tightly to a round frame with a long handle
referee	/refərˈiː/	(n)	a person who is in charge of a sports game and who makes certain that the rules are followed
ring	/rɪŋ/	(n)	a special area where people perform or compete
rink	/rɪŋk/	(n)	a large, flat surface made of ice or wood where you can skate/move wearing boots with wheels or a piece of metal
score	/skɔː/	(n)	the number of points someone gets in a game or test
skate	/skeɪt/	(n)	a special boot with a thin metal bar or wheels fixed to the bottom that you wear to move quickly on ice or a hard surface
tennis	/ˈtenɪs/	(n)	a sport in which two or four people hit a small ball to each other over a net
vest	/vest/	(n)	a piece of clothing with buttons at the front and no sleeves, that you wear over a shirt
yet	/jet/	(adv)	up until now

Vocabulary	Pronunciation	Part of speech	Definition
UNIT 8			
anxious	/ˈæŋkʃəs/	(adj)	worried and nervous
bad	/bæd/	(adj)	unpleasant; causing difficulties or harm
best	/best/	(adj)	(superlative of good) better than any other
boring	/ˈbɔːrɪŋ/	(adj)	not interesting or exciting
business	/ˈbɪznɪs/	(n)	an organization that sells goods or services
calm	/kɑːm/	(adj)	relaxed and not worried, frightened, or excited
careful	/ˈkeəfəl/	(adj)	giving a lot of attention to what you are doing so that you do not have an accident, make a mistake, or damage something
careless	/ˈkeələs/	(adj)	not giving enough attention to what you are doing
carry on (with)	/ˈkæri ɒn wɪð/	(v)	continue
driving licence	/draɪvɪŋ ˈlaɪsənts/	(n)	official permission for someone to drive a car, received after passing a driving test, or a document showing this
earn	/ɜːn/	(v)	to get money for doing work
excellent	/ˈeksələnt/	(adj)	extremely good
experience	/ɪkˈspɪəriənts/	(n)	knowledge that you get from doing a job, or from doing, seeing, or feeling something
find (sth) out	/faɪnd aʊt/	(v)	to get information about something
get by	/get baɪ/	(v)	to deal with a situation by having just enough of something
get on (with)	/get ɒn wɪð/	(v)	to start or continue doing something, especially work
half	/hɑːf/	(n)	one of two equal parts of something
job title	/dʒɒb ˈtaɪtəl/	(n)	the name of a particular job in an organization
learn	/lɜːn/	(v)	to get knowledge or skill in a new subject or activity
look after sb/sth	/lʊk ˈɑːftər/	(v)	to take care of or be in charge of someone or something
look at	/lʊk ət/	(v)	to direct your eyes in order to see something
manager	/ˈmænɪdʒə/	(n)	someone in control of an office, shop, team, etc.
note down	/nəʊt daʊn/	(v)	to write something so that you do not forget it
per cent	/pəˈsent/	(adv)	for or out of every 100, shown by the symbol %
personal quality	/ˈpɜːsənəl ˈkwɒləti/	(n)	a good feature of a person's character
point	/pɔɪnt/	(v)	to show where someone or something is by holding your finger or a thin object towards it
practice	/ˈpræktɪs/	(n)	when you repeat an activity to improve your ability
qualification	/kwɒlɪfɪˈkeɪʃən/	(n)	something that you get when you are successful in an exam or course of study
real	/rɪəl/	(adj)	not artificial or false
run out of	/rʌn aʊt ɒv/	(v)	to not have enough of something
ship	/ʃɪp/	(n)	a large boat that carries people or goods by sea
single	/ˈsɪŋgəl/	(adj)	not married, or not having a romantic relationship with someone
sink	/sɪŋk/	(v)	to go down or make something go down below the surface of water or a soft substance and not come back up
smart	/smɑːt/	(adj)	having a clean, tidy and stylish appearance
spend time	/spend taɪm/	(phr)	use time doing something
storm	/stɔːm/	(n)	very bad weather with a lot of rain, snow, wind, etc.
take part	/teɪk pɑːt/	(v)	to be involved in an activity with other people
take up	/ˈteɪkʌp/	(v)	to start doing a particular job or activity
untidy	/ʌnˈtaɪdi/	(adj)	not tidy
upset	/ʌpˈset/	(adj)	unhappy or worried because something unpleasant has happened
worst	/wɜːst/	(adj)	(superlative of bad) the most unpleasant, difficult or severe

Vocabulary	Pronunciation	Part of speech	Definition
UNIT 9			
bag	/bæg/	(n)	a container made of paper, plastic, leather, etc., used for carrying things
believable	/bɪˈliːvəbəl/	(adj)	If something is believable, you can believe that it could be true or real.
belt	/belt/	(n)	a long, thin piece of material that you wear around your waist
bored / boring	/bɔːd / bɔːrɪŋ/	(adj)	not feeling interested or excited
broom	/bruːm/	(n)	a brush with a long handle used for cleaning the floor
bucket	/ˈbʌkɪt/	(n)	a container with an open top and a handle, often used for carrying liquids
circular	/ˈsɜːkjələ/	(adj)	shaped like a circle
comb	/kəʊm/	(n)	used to tidy and arrange your hair
comfortable	/ˈkʌmpftəbəl/	(adj)	describes furniture, clothes, etc. that provide a pleasant feeling and that do not give you any pain
diamond-shaped	/ˈdaɪəmənd ʃeɪpt/	(adj)	having the shape of a diamond
emperor	/ˈempərə/	(n)	the male ruler of an empire
encyclopaedia	/ɪnsaɪkləˈpiːdiə/	(n)	a book or set of articles containing many items arranged in alphabetical order that deal either with the whole of human knowledge or one particular subject
excited / exciting	/ɪkˈsaɪtɪd / ɪkˈsaɪtɪŋ/	(adj)	feeling very happy and enthusiastic
expensive	/ɪkˈspentsɪv/	(adj)	costing a lot of money
extraordinary	/ɪkˈstrɔːdənəri/	(adj)	very special, unusual or strange
fascinated / fascinating	/ˈfæsɪneɪtɪd / ˈfæsɪneɪtɪŋ/	(adj)	very interested / very interesting
funeral	/ˈfjuːnərəl/	(n)	a ceremony for burying or burning the body of a dead person
handle	/ˈhændəl/	(n)	the part of something that you use to hold it or open it
headphones	/ˈhedfəʊnz/	(n)	You wear these over your ears so that you can listen to music.
homeless	/ˈhəʊmləs/	(adj)	without a home
interested / interesting	/ˈɪntrəstɪd / ˈɪntrəstɪŋ/	(adj)	not bored / boring
invent	/ɪnˈvent/	(v)	to design or create something which has never existed before
invention	/ɪnˈventʃən/	(n)	something which has been designed or created for the first time, or the act of creating or designing something
lamp	/læmp/	(n)	a piece of equipment that produces light
length	/leŋkθ/	(n)	the measurement or distance of something
made of	/meɪd ɒv/	(phr)	to describe what material is used for something
metal	/ˈmetəl/	(n)	a usually hard, shiny material such as iron, gold, or silver which heat and electricity can travel through
mug	/mʌg/	(n)	a large cup with straight sides used for hot drinks
oval	/ˈəʊvəl/	(adj)	in the shape of an egg or a slightly flat circle
plastic	/ˈplæstɪk/	(n)	a light, artificial substance that can be made into different shapes when it is soft and is used in a lot of different ways
polite	/pəˈlaɪt/	(adj)	behaving in a way that is not rude and shows that you do not only think about yourself
rectangular	/rekˈtæŋgjələ/	(adj)	shaped like a rectangle, with four 90° angles, four sides, with opposite sides of equal length and two sides longer than the other two
relaxed / relaxing	/rɪˈlækst / rɪˈlæksɪŋ/	(adj)	feeling happy and comfortable because nothing is worrying you
remarkable	/rɪˈmɑːkəbəl/	(adj)	very unusual or noticeable in a way that you admire
round	/raʊnd/	(adj)	in the shape of a circle or ball
ruler	/ruːlə/	(n)	a flat, straight stick which is used to measure things

Vocabulary	Pronunciation	Part of speech	Definition
shocked / shocking	/ʃɒkt / ʃɒkɪŋ/	(adj)	to make someone feel upset or surprised
successful	/sək'sesfəl/	(adj)	achieving what you want to achieve
surprised / surprising	/sə'praɪzd / sə'praɪzɪŋ/	(adj)	feeling or showing surprise because something has happened that you did not expect
sword	/sɔːd/	(n)	a weapon with a long, metal blade and a handle
tiring / tired	/taɪərɪŋ / taɪəd/	(adj)	in need of rest or sleep
triangular	/traɪ'æŋgjələ/	(adj)	shaped like a triangle
used to	/juːzd tuː/	(v)	to put something such as a tool, skill, or building to a particular purpose
weight	/weɪt/	(n)	the amount that something or someone weighs
wheelbarrow	/'hwiːlbærəʊ/	(n)	a big, open container with a wheel at the front and handles that is used to move things
wind	/waɪnd/	(v)	to turn a handle or knob on a device (e.g. a clock or watch) to make it work
UNIT 10			
astronomy	/ə'strɒnəmi/	(n)	the scientific study of stars and planets
by / on water	/baɪ / ɒn 'wɔːtə/	(phr)	to go on a boat or ship
conference	/'kɒnfərənts/	(n)	a large, formal meeting, often lasting a few days, where people discuss their work, politics, subjects they are studying, etc.
couple	/'kʌpəl/	(n)	two or a few
cruise	/kruːz/	(n)	a holiday on a large ship, sailing from place to place
diamond	/'daɪə.mənd /	(n)	a transparent, extremely hard precious stone that is used in jewellery
exploration	/eksplə'reɪʃən/	(n)	a journey to a place to find out about something
explore	/ɪk'splɔː/	(v)	to go around a place where you have never been in order to find out what is there
explorer	/ɪk'splɔːrə/	(n)	someone who travels to places where no one has ever been in order to find out what is there
flight	/flaɪt/	(n)	a journey through air or space in an aircraft or other vehicle
fly	/flaɪ/	(v)	to travel through the air in an aircraft
journey	/'dʒɜːni/	(n)	when you travel from one place to another
present	/pre'zənt/	(v)	to give people information in a formal way
presentation	/prezən'teɪʃən/	(n)	a talk giving information about something
presenter	/prə'zentə/	(n)	someone who introduces a television or radio show
project	/prɒ'dʒekt/	(n)	a study of a particular subject done over a period of time
research	/rɪ'sɜːtʃ/	(v)	to study a subject in detail or to try to find information about a subject
research	/'riːɜːtʃ/	(n)	when someone studies a subject in detail or tries to find information about a subject
researcher	/rɪ'sɜːtʃə/	(n)	someone who does research as a job
space	/speɪs/	(n)	the area outside the Earth's atmosphere, where the planets and the stars are
travel	/'trævəl/	(n)	the activity of travelling
travel	/'trævəl/	(v)	to make a journey
traveller	/'trævələ/	(n)	someone who travels
trip	/trɪp/	(n)	a journey in which you visit a place for a short time and come back
voyage	/'vɔɪɪdʒ/	(n)	a long journey, especially by ship, or in space
whether	/'weðə/	(conj)	used especially in reporting questions and when expressing doubt to mean if
work	/wɜːk/	(n)	when you use physical or mental effort to do something
worker	/wɜːkə/	(n)	someone who works for a company or organization but does not have a powerful position

VIDEO AND AUDIO SCRIPTS

UNIT 1

▶ Living in Alaska

Narrator: Alaska: the largest state in the United States of America. It has the fewest people living in it, with a population of only 722,000 people. Why do so few people live here? One reason is the long winter. Winter lasts eight months in Alaska. In some places the temperature can drop as low as -60° celsius. Everyone is waiting for winter to come: the people, wolves, bears and moose.

Kachemak Bay is on the Kenai Peninsula on the south coast of Alaska.

People in this part of Alaska live from the land. They are not close to shops or other services that are normally in towns. And they don't go to the supermarket and buy food from the shelves.

The Kilcher family has lived in the bay for many years. They know that they have to prepare their home for the long winter. They have to chop wood and save it for the winter months. It is important to store the pieces of wood next to their house because in winter there is too much snow to do this job. The wood is used for fuel to heat the house for the whole of the winter. The wood is put into a fire called a stove. The stove is in the middle of the kitchen.

Another job to do before winter is to move all their cows. In the summer months the cows live in Kachemak bay. But the men must move the cows before winter comes. Moving the cows is called, 'driving the cattle home'. It is not an easy job. The two brothers, Otto and Atz, have to get the cattle home before the weather gets too bad.

It is also important to collect all the vegetables from the garden. The vegetables are put into boxes and stored in the house to keep them safe. They store fruit in cans and jars.

A big storm is coming. Brothers Otto and Atz are still driving the cattle home. The brothers will have to spend the night outdoors. Atz's son Atz Lee is worried.

Winter has come early. Luckily, Otto and Atz make it home with the cattle after two days and everyone is safe.

🔊 1.1

1 place
2 hot
3 quick
4 up

🔊 1.2

James: Welcome to the Travel Podcast. I'm James, I'm here with Suzzy and today we're looking at unusual places where people actually live. Suzzy, have you seen any unusual homes around the world?

Suzzy: Well it depends what you mean by unusual. I live in a detached house, so the tenement buildings in New York, for example, seem pretty unusual to me.

James: I really mean places which very few people know about …

Suzzy: Oh, I see … Erm. Well, when I was on holiday last year in Yemen, I saw some tall flats made from mud. You could say they are unusual.

James: Yes, they are very unusual! And so are the cave houses at a place called Matmata.

Suzzy: Matmata? Is that in Egypt?

James: No, it's in Tunisia. Have a look at the picture. You might recognize it from the *Star Wars* films. They filmed some of the scenes there. But actually these houses in the caves are real. People started living in them 700 years ago. They made them out of the rock.

Suzzy: Wow! That's ancient! Where exactly is it?

James: It's about 355 kilometres south of the capital, Tunis. I'd love to go there. Actually, when I was younger I went to Cappadocia in Turkey. It was fantastic! There are cave houses there too. It's in Anatolia in the centre of Turkey. Have a look.

Suzzy: The buildings look like mushrooms!

James: Strange place isn't it? The houses formed from rock over 8,000 years ago. People changed them into homes during the Roman period. Some people still live there now.

Suzzy: Now? That's amazing. But did you know that some people live on bridges? Look at these two pictures.

James: Oh yes. This one is beautiful and it looks very old. It's in Italy isn't it? Is it Rome?

Suzzy: Well it is in Italy. It is called the Ponte Vecchio but it's actually in Florence, north of Rome. They built the bridge in 1345. There was another bridge there before but an accident destroyed it. So they made this one and people started to live there. It's lovely isn't it?

James: The bridge in the other picture looks newer.

Suzzy: Yes that's Neft Dashlari in Azerbaijan.

James: Where?

Suzzy: Azerbaijan. You know- A-Z-E-R-B-A-I-J-A-N.

James: Oh, ok. It looks really long and industrial. Do people work there?

Suzzy: Yes, they drill for oil from under the sea there. They decided that the workers needed somewhere to live so they built a kind of 'city' above the sea. The bridge is 30 miles long. They put houses, libraries, schools and even a cinema there.

James: Really? So hundreds of people live there?

Suzzy: 5,000 people live there. It even appeared in a *James Bond* film.

James: Well it makes my house look very boring!

Suzzy: And mine!

🔊 1.3

Teacher: Ok everyone. Today we are talking about going places, getting around easily. Now in the past if you wanted to go places you would use a map. But nowadays we use one of these …

Satnav: Exit ahead. In 800 metres, take the left exit. Exit ahead. Take the next exit then keep on the right.

Teacher: Sound familiar? Who has a car here? Ok. And who has a satnav? So that is most of us. Obviously, satnavs are now in most new cars. As we know, they give us directions while we drive and we can also look at the pictures or images of the route or the way we want to go. But how many of you know what satnav means and how they work? Satnav is short for satellite navigation but it is also called a GPS system. They were made first in 1978 and now use 24 satellites to find out where a car is located. So, now you have the facts, I'd like to talk about the advantages and disadvantages of satnavs. I'd also like to give you an idea of some of the research that has been done on satnavs.

First of all, let's look at the advantages of satnavs. I think most of us know how dangerous and difficult it is to try to read a map while driving. It's also very time-consuming to stop the car every time we need to look at a map. This is why a GPS takes the stress out of driving. Some GPS systems can even tell drivers where the traffic is bad, which explains why the majority of us think satnavs are great.

But I'd also like to talk about disadvantages. Some scientists have found that satnavs can be dangerous and cause accidents. Why do scientists think this? Well, research shows us the brain takes time to process information, especially things that we see. So if a driver looks at the satnav picture, their brain is still working on this picture as they drive on. This means they are thinking about the satnav picture, not the road in front of them. So scientists can show there is more chance of the driver having an accident.

Now I think that this may be true. But I also believe that our journeys are more complicated than this. Most drivers use a satnav when they are going to a new area or on a trip or a tour. They don't use it every day. So they don't actually know the roads very well and this might also cause accidents. And I personally feel that most drivers listen to a satnav rather than look. In my opinion, the pictures on the satnav are not important. It seems to me that drivers don't actually look at the satnav very often.

Finally, the advantages of satnavs, in my opinion are greater than the disadvantages. We can all see that the GPS makes driving easier. Accidents are very bad but they can happen at any time. And we don't know how many people had accidents in the past because they were looking at a map. So I will continue to use my GPS. But I'd like to know what you think?

🔊 **1.4**

1   I'd like to talk about about the advantages and disadvantages of satnavs.

2   First of all, let's look at the advantages.

3   I'd also like to talk about some disadvantages.

4   Finally, the advantages of satnavs, in my opinion are greater than the disadvantages.

🔊 **1.5**

I'd like to talk about the advantages and disadvantages of satnavs.

🔊 **1.6**

First of all let's look at the advantages.

UNIT 2

▶ A Chinese New Year

Festivals are celebrated around the world. In China, people are getting ready to celebrate one of the world's biggest festivals. This is Chinese New Year. For 15 days in spring, 800 million people travel across China to be with their friends and family. People decorate their homes with red lanterns. They paint red paper banners with good luck phrases like 'Happiness' and 'Wealth' and hang them outside the front door.

Across the country, there are parades in every town. People wear bright costumes, dance and play music. In the famous dragon dance, young men carry a dragon made of paper, silk and wood in the air and dance through the streets, collecting money.

On New Year's Eve, everyone sits down together for a traditional meal with their family. This meal has 22 courses. They exchange gifts of money, put inside a red envelope for luck. People also take small gifts of food to their friends, like oranges or sweets. At night, the streets fill with people.

But no Chinese New Year celebration is complete without fireworks. All across the country, the New Year is welcomed with firework displays big and small. One of the biggest displays is in the city of Hong Kong. Over one million people come to watch the display, which uses several tonnes of fireworks.

🔊 **2.1**

Presenter: Today I am at the Festival of Ideas, which has happened in the UK each October since 2008. It is a free festival with lots of activities organized by the University of Cambridge. But it isn't just for students. Anyone interested in Art and Science can go to the lectures, talks, classes and performances. The festival has become bigger every year; the first year, 7000 people attended but by the third year that number was almost double. We asked one of the visitors about the festival.

Presenter :   Hello there. Is this your first time at the festival here in Cambridge?

Woman 1:   Oh no, I come here every year!

Presenter: Can you tell us about why you like coming to the festival?

Woman 1:   Yes of course! It is an interesting event to come to. It's great for kids and adults. I love learning about all the new ideas people have on important topics. We don't get much time to really think or learn new things in everyday life but you can do it at this festival.

Presenter: So what kind of things do people learn?

Woman 1:   Well, today I did some history. I learnt about traditional British Tudor dance, the sort Henry VIII did, and everyone tried one of the dances. It was really good fun! The day before I played games to find out about gravity. It was a Science activity. And tomorrow I'm going to a lecture on the global economy, which will really make me think!

Presenter: Are there any things you don't like about it? Are you ever bored?

Woman 1: Not really. The only problem is that it is very crowded!

Presenter: This visitor, like many others, is really enjoying the Festival of Ideas. Nowadays there are more and more new festivals, often based on music, food or culture, around the world. Take Iceland Airwaves for example …

Presenter: Iceland Airwaves is another festival held in October. This one started in 1999 and is held in the capital of Iceland, Reykjavik. Isak works at the festival. Hi Isak.

Man: Hi. Welcome to Iceland Airwaves!

Presenter: Thanks. So what happens here?

Man: Well as you can hear, it is a music festival. We have many bands from all over the world and we try to present new and interesting music.

Presenter: Have you got many people here from other countries?

Man: Yes. Our visitors are from all over the world. As well as the music there are lots of clubs and people can go sightseeing too. There are some beautiful natural places and lots of museums to visit. I think it is the best music festival around now!

Presenter: Well I hope you enjoy the rest of the event! Visiting such festivals is not just for entertainment, it is a fantastic way to find out about the culture of a different country.

Presenter: Nasrra is visiting the Muscat Festival with her family. This is held in January and February each year in Oman and Nasrra has been coming for the last couple of years. Hi Nasrra. Are you enjoying the festival?

Woman 2: Yes! It is wonderful!

Presenter: Can you tell us something about the festival?

Woman 2: Of course. It is a chance for people to learn about the heritage and culture of Oman.

Presenter: So why are you here?

Woman 2: My mother and father want to watch some of the sport; there was cycling last year and also a camel race. You can also learn traditional dance. But I want to go to the fashion show.

Presenter: That sounds great.

Woman 2: Yes. And after we will go and eat some traditional food …

Presenter: So these international festivals with lots of music, food, dance and fashion are providing a different type of experience for people.

2.2

Woman 1: It is an interesting event to come to.

2.3

1 … what kind of things do people do?
2 Are there any things you don't like …?
3 Have you got many people here from other countries?

2.4

Presenter: Thanks for coming to tell us about the food festival starting this weekend David, it sounds great. Before you tell us about it can I ask how long you have been doing the festival?

David: This is our second year.

Presenter: Great. And do you like your job?

David: Yes, I love it. I have always been interested in food so it is a great job for me.

Presenter: Are you a chef?

David: No, but I like cooking.

Presenter: So, tell us about the event. What time does the festival start?

David: At 10 o'clock this Saturday.

Presenter: What kinds of food do you have?

David: Anything local: bread, vegetables, meat, that kind of thing.

Presenter: Is it all good?

David: Yes, it is fantastic.

Presenter: Where do people eat their lunch? Are the people coming here to buy food or eat it?

David: Both really. We have some small cafes where people can have lunch.

Presenter: Finally, is the work interesting?

David: Very interesting. Come on Saturday and see why!

2.5

Teacher: Hello everyone. Today's lesson on culture is about wedding celebrations and food. The information is all in the infographics poster which I will email you after the lesson. But you could look at this online now if you have a tablet or phone with you. Before we look at the first picture, I'd like you to think about a wedding in your country. What would you probably eat? I am sure everyone here will have a good idea because in most countries there are some special dishes which people always have at weddings.

So how about starting with wedding cake? Have a look at this beautiful cake here. You could try this at weddings in countries such as Australia, the USA, the UK and many others. It is usually made with dried fruit although nowadays some people prefer different kinds such as chocolate. Most traditional Western cakes are white and have three or four layers with beautiful decorations like flowers made from sugar. This is one of the many customs which date back to many years ago in England. In medieval times, wedding cakes were put in layers until they were very tall and the new husband and wife would kiss over the cake. If they did this without the cake falling people believed they would have a good marriage. Other things used to make the cakes look nice are little models of the man and woman getting married which are put on the top.

This type of wedding cake is becoming popular in other countries around the world but with some differences. In Bermuda, for instance, the couple have two cakes, one for the bride and one for the groom. Have a look at this next image. You can see they put a tiny tree on the top of each cake to show that they will grow like a tree.

But not all wedding meals are sweet. In Korea, for example, couples have long noodles called kuk soo. They are long because they show everyone the long life that the couple will have together. In Ghana, in Africa, there is a special meal just for the woman. Brides there always eat oto, a traditional food, on the morning of the wedding. This dish is made from mixing yams, a vegetable a bit like sweet potato, with oil or butter and is always eaten with eggs. How about having that before you get married? Brides in Ghana do this because they have to stand for a long time during the wedding day and it helps them to be strong.

In Morocco, people like to have a traditional tagine. This is meat with a sauce, cooked in a pot with a special lid. It takes a long time to cook and the same pot is passed around for everyone to share. You can get tagine in good Moroccan restaurants. Why not try it yourself?

🔊 **2.6**

1 ... nowadays some people prefer different kinds, such as chocolate.
2 Most traditional Western cakes have three or four layers with beautiful decorations , like flowers made from sugar.
3 In Bermuda, for instance, the couple have two cakes.
4 In Korea, for example, couples have long noodles called kuk soo.

UNIT 3

▶ Education around the world

Narrator: This is morning in a primary school in China. The children are having assembly. This is when the teachers check that all the children are at school and call out the names of the children in their class. Each class has about 37 students.

This is Wushu City in China, a town that is famous for training in martial arts. There are schools like this all over the town, with thousands of students. The students live in very simple rooms with no heating. They get up at five in the morning and the training is very difficult. Children and teenagers travel here from all over China for one reason: to get a job. Getting a certificate from one of these schools can get them a job in the army, as a security guard, or in the police. All well-paid jobs for life, but they must work very hard to complete their education first.

This is a boarding school in India. The boys live, sleep and eat here. They take the same lessons as any other Indian school; from maths, to geography and languages. Without families, the boys make friends quickly, Anuj says he has exactly 106 friends! This school gives them hope for the future.

In this village in South Africa, children like Thobela Sohobese walks ten kilometres a day to school. Thobela is 14 years old. Thobela's school doesn't have many text books. So the teacher uses newspapers. The teacher hopes that his students will get good jobs. Thobela wants to be the first person in her family to go to high school and university. She hopes to become a teacher. The school has a kitchen and feeds three hundred children each day. For many of them, it is their only hot meal. At home, Thobela and her brothers and sister eat together. After dinner Thobela does her homework. ... She is studying for her end-of-year exams.

It is the day of the exam results. Thobela has passed. She is very happy because she wants to find a good job when she is older and help her parents.

🔊 **3.1**

Josh: Welcome everyone.

Ali, Karina and Akiko: Hello / hi

Josh: Good to see you all today and I hope you will enjoy this part of your visit to the university. I'm here to show you around some of the main places on campus. My name's Josh, and as you can hear, I'm American. The manager of the international office asked me to show you around the campus because I'm an international student like you and I know what it's like trying to settle into a new country and learn a whole new university system. If you have any questions at all while we're walking round, please just ask.

Ali: Ok thanks.

Josh: Right... here is a map for everyone. Have a look now. We are in front of the stairs in the main hall. Can you see it here on the map?

Akiko: Yes I see.

Josh: The canteen where you can have lunch is opposite the stairs. It's self-service, so don't expect a waiter to come to your table. On the right, next to the canteen, is the international office.

Akiko: Did you say near the canteen?

Josh: Right next to it, to the right side. Can you see?

Josh: Oh yes.

Josh: You can get lots of help and information there. It's a really useful place to go for help with visas or advice about your studies. Just to the left of the canteen is the events office. This is where you can find out about all the social events and activities. There is a lot going on outside of your lectures. Music and sport clubs, theatre and politics societies. I've made a lot of good friends by joining clubs.

Karina: Mmm, great.

Josh: And can you see the corridor just past the international office?

Ali: Yes.

Josh: The first room on the left is the library. You can borrow books there or make photocopies of the pages you need. The second room on the left is a computer room. You get free internet access 24 hours a day if you show your university ID card. And opposite them is a lecture theatre. I think it is used for Geography and History lectures. Are any of you planning to study Science at all?

Akiko: Yes. I'm going to take Biology.

Josh: Ok. Well we will need to go upstairs then. The science laboratories are on the first floor. So if you would all like to follow me ...So, here's one of the laboratories. You can have a look around if you like, but please don't touch anything.

Ali: Wow! What a huge laboratory. Look at all this equipment! Do you study science, Josh?

Josh: No, I study French and Art. I'll show you the classrooms where we have seminars later. They're in a building on the other side of the campus.

Ali: OK. Are you enjoying your course?

Josh: Yes I love it! My professors are really good- sorry- I mean lecturers. In the US we say teacher, lecturer or professor and they all mean the same thing, but here they are all a bit different. Not all the lecturers are professors …

🔊 **3.2**

1   Yes that's true.

2   Yes that's true.

🔊 **3.3**

1   Yes I enjoyed most of it.

2   I agree.

3   It was ok I suppose.

4   I agree …

🔊 **3.4**

Tutor: Ok everyone, before the tutorial I asked you to think about the ways people learn nowadays and how you feel about them. Today I'd like you to share your opinions and experiences of learning with technology. Sarah would you like to start?

Sarah: Well, I've tried learning online. I did an online Maths course last year. I've always found maths quite difficult so I thought this would be a good way to improve.

Nazlihan: Did you like it?

Sarah: Yes I enjoyed most of it, but I am not sure it helped me that much. I think I would find it better to work with a teacher, you know, in a traditional class. Because when I found something difficult I really wanted a teacher there to explain it to me.

Tutor: What do you think Peter?

Peter: About online learning? Well for me it's great; you can work at the speed you want. You can go back and look at things again. I think it really works.

Tutor: You don't look sure Nazlihan?

Nazlihan: Well I have never done online courses. I probably agree with Sarah: I prefer to have a teacher there to help me. I see what Peter is saying...but I am not sure really.

Peter: Nazlihan, you know that online courses often have an online teacher who can answer questions. Isn't that the same thing in a way? For me it's better because you have time to think about what help you want too.

Nazlihan: Yes, but on the other hand it isn't the same as speaking to someone and asking them to repeat things like with a real teacher.

Tutor: Have you done anything with computers Nazlihan?

Nazlihan: Well last year we did some stuff in the computer rooms at the college. There was a language course and everyone went to the computer rooms once a week. It was ok I suppose, but to be honest I just didn't find it very helpful.

Peter: Was it really online though? Or was it just doing exercises on a computer?

Nazlihan: Probably a lot of exercises really. So for me it didn't work well. But I've been learning new vocabulary on my smart phone since then. And I love doing that! It's really helpful.

Sarah: Yes that's true Nazlihan! Mobile learning is great- you can do it whenever you want- even on the bus.

Peter: I agree Sarah, I mean I agree that it is convenient but I don't like the small screen.

Tutor: Of course the type of learning we haven't talked about is blended learning: using technology and traditional classroom learning together. We do it on this course all the time!

Sarah: For me blended learning is the best way to learn. I think you get help from the teacher but you can also do interesting work using technology to support you too. So you get two kinds of help. It's true, I am not saying it because you are here!

Nazlihan: I think you are right.

Peter: And me.

Tutor: Well that is good to hear...but why do you think …

UNIT 4

▶ Virtual reality

Narrator: Diving is a popular activity to do in your free time or on holiday, but it can be expensive. To dive, you need special clothes, tools and training and the best places to dive are often far away. But now, a team of scientists is using virtual reality so that everyone can go diving from their own home.

Usually, you have to wear a helmet to see virtual reality, but with this technology your whole body is used. The glasses can tell where you are standing, so it feels like what you are seeing is really there.

This technology means that people can swim with sharks safely, and without getting special training, inside a normal swimming pool.

The scientists will use this shark tank for testing. The team put a mini submarine and a camera in the shark tank. The cables send a picture of the sharks back to a screen. Happy that the camera works, they must next see if they can project the image.

The team put the screen into a swimming pool. In the control room, they start the projector. Back at the shark tank, they get the camera ready. They cover the swimming pool and the first viewing starts. In the swimming pool the video from the shark tank can be seen clearly. It's amazing that with the right technology, you can now swim with sharks anywhere.

🔊 **4.1**

Presenter: Welcome to University Radio, the station run by students for students. I'm Chen Hu and this is Science Today. Our subject is technological development and our guest is Professor James Holden, expert in robotics. Thanks for coming in Professor. When we think of robots we generally think of science fiction films. Is this out of date?

Professor: Yes it is. Technology has developed very fast over the last ten years and robots are very much a fact of everyday life. Robots can now do many important things.

Presenter: What kind of things?

Professor: Well they have been used in factories for years; Japan and China have the most industrial robots in the world. But now robots are coming into our lives in other ways. In Japan, Thailand and Hong Kong for example there are robot waiters in restaurants, and in South Korea a robot is used as an English teacher. Robots weren't used so much in the past as they were always very expensive. But as they have become cheaper they are being used in new and interesting ways. Another key area is the way robots can help with medical care.

Presenter: Can you explain a bit more?

Professor: Well, a good example is the robotic suit for disabled people. Robots can now assist people who can't walk. They can help them to move again. People 'wear' the robot, like clothes. The robot then helps move the person's legs or arms. For example, one man, Joey Abbica, couldn't walk because of an accident at work three years earlier. Before the accident, Joey could surf very well. In fact, he won lots of competitions, but straight after the accident he couldn't walk at all. He wasn't even able to sit up on his own when a visitor came. And he couldn't even feel his legs when doctors touched them. But when he put on the robotic suit he was able to stand up and to walk on his own again. He isn't able to walk at all without the suit. Robotics has changed his life.

Presenter: So people have a much better quality of life thanks to these new types of robot?

Professor: Yes that's right. Service robots are also very helpful to people.

Presenter: What do service robots do?

Professor: Well, one of the reasons that service robots were invented is to save people time. They do all the jobs around the house that people find difficult, dirty or boring. For instance robots can put clothes into a washing machine, plates and cups into a dishwasher, they can clean your kitchen and bathroom. But for some people, service robots are very important, they're not just a luxury. Old people, for example, can't always do housework easily. They need help from robots, because of their age. The robot means they are able to stay in their own homes for longer.

Presenter: So robots can help people in their everyday life but how do they help more generally?

Professor: Robots are now solving modern problems too. Have you heard of robotic fish?

Presenter: I haven't but I guess they are robots that swim in water? What do they do?

Professor: They were developed to check the pollution levels in sea water. They look like fish, they swim and move like other fish, but when they are swimming they can collect information about the amount of pollution in the water. We can find out about the pollution quickly due to the robot fish.

Presenter: Well I have heard of robots that clean your house so it is good to know they can help keep the environment clean too. Ok, we have had some questions coming in so let's have a look at the first one …

🔊 **4.2**

Newsreader: For a long time people have asked the same question: do computers stop us learning and developing? Do they make us stupid? A recent study at Columbia University in America has been looking at this question, in particular how computers affect our memory. They wanted to find out if computers have changed the way we remember information.

Firstly the scientists researched what happens when people are asked difficult questions. They found that what we think when we hear difficult questions has changed due to websites like Google™. When people were asked difficult questions in the past scientists believe they tried to think of the answer to the question. However, because of modern websites, the first thing people think about now is how to find the answer; they don't try to answer it themselves. For example they think about what they might put into Google™, whereas in the past they thought about the question itself.

Secondly scientists found that computers have changed the type of information we remember. There are advantages and disadvantages to these changes. Firstly a disadvantage. It seems that people now forget facts especially if they know the information will be saved in a computer file. On the other hand, an advantage is that they remember the location of the fact; in other words where to find it. In one test, scientists told university students some facts and also where the facts were saved on a computer file. Most of the students couldn't remember the facts but they were able to remember the files and location of the fact.

In conclusion, it seems that computers are not making us stupid but they are making us lazy! Scientists believe that we are spending time remembering where and how we can find things but we are not trying to remember the information itself anymore.

🔊 **4.3**

1 When people were asked difficult questions in the past scientists believe they tried to think of the answer to the question. However because of modern websites, the first thing people think about now is how to find the answer.

2 For example they think about what they might put into Google™, whereas in the past they thought about the question itself.

3 It seems that people now forget facts especially if they know the information will be saved in a computer file. On the other hand an advantage is they remember the location of the fact and where to find it.

4 In conclusion, it seems that computers are not making us stupid but they are making us lazy!

UNIT 5

▶ Languages in South America

Narrator: South America is one of the most interesting places in the world. It has 12 countries and nearly 400 million people. Some parts are very hot; other parts are cold and mountainous. There are rivers and lakes where people travel and work. There are places with few people and big cities where many people live.

Communicating in a place as big as South America is not easy. It reaches from the Equator to Antarctica.The Caribbean Sea is in the north. To the east is the Atlantic Ocean and the Pacific Ocean is in the west.

How do all the people in these different places talk to each other? The languages used most are Spanish and Portuguese but there are many other languages too.

Brazil is the biggest country in South America, famous for the city of Rio and its beautiful beaches. Almost all the people of Brazil speak Portuguese. But some also speak Guarani, a local language passed on from the people who lived in Brazil thousands of years ago.

Colombia is the second biggest country in South America and is home to cities like Bogotá. Most Colombians speak Spanish. But a few hundred people still speak a language called Uitoto. In fact Colombia once had 68 other languages but only a few of them remain.

Argentinians are also mostly Spanish speakers. A million and a half of the people speak Italian too. And, just like Brazil and Colombia, there are some local languages that have been spoken for thousands of years. Some, like Vilela, only have 15 or 20 speakers left.

But why is it that these old languages are not as popular as Spanish and Portuguese?

Over 500 years ago, Europeans from Spain and Portugal arrived in South America just before 1500. They soon introduced their own languages. But before the Spanish and Portuguese came, there were many different people already living in South America, speaking hundreds of different languages.

Some people still live in the same way as their ancestors did hundreds of years ago. They still speak the same languages.

The ancient cities and places where these languages started have mostly gone now. A few are left but they are not busy any more. They are places for tourists to visit, like Machu Picchu in The Andes Mountains. Many people hope that the same thing doesn't happen to the old languages of South America. They hope that people will continue to speak them.

◀))) 5.1

1 You should learn English!
2 Come and learn with us!
3 Don't forget to study!

◀))) 5.2

1 Come and learn with us!
2 You should learn English!
3 We can help!
4 Come to us for lessons!

◀))) 5.3

1

Presenter: And finally, a report today from the Endangered Language Project says that over 50% of the languages we speak will be gone in the next 80 years. Language specialists from all over the world have joined the project to try and make sure that rare languages are protected.

At the moment there are around 7000 different languages in the world. But today's report shows that many of these languages are spoken by fewer and fewer people. Recently the last speaker of a language called Bo died at the age of 85. The woman, Boa Senior, who lived in the Indian Andaman islands, learnt to communicate using Hindi because no one else could speak her language. She was the last woman in the world who understood Bo, one of the world's most ancient languages. Professor Anvita Abbi said the world had lost an important part of Indian culture and language tradition with her death.

If you want to know more about Bo, visit our website and download the factsheet on endangered languages. Now let's hear about today's weather…

2

Professor Kassis' answerphone: Hello. This is the answer phone for Professor Kassis. Please leave your name, number and a message after the beep and I'll call you back.

Jose Torres: Hello Professor. This is Jose Torres, a student in your department. I am doing some research on unusual languages spoken in the USA and I wanted to ask you for some information. I know that you have done some work on the Navajo language. I am studying the history of Navajo at the moment— I don't speak it myself but I know only 5% of Navajo children can use it now and so I wanted to find out more about the background. I hope you can help me with this. Can you call me back when you get this message? My number is 385 383 449 Thanks very much. Bye.

3

Museum tour guide: Follow me if you wouldn't mind. Right, here we are in the Russian and Mongolian sections. In fact we will begin with Tuva, which is located in a very distant part of Russia near Mongolia. If you look here you can see some musical instruments from Tuva. This two stringed instrument is called an Igil. The body of this one is made of wood, but they're sometimes covered with a goat skin. They're often decorated with a horse's head because of the connection with an old folk tale which tells of a boy who rescues a horse. The Tuvan area is famous for 'throat singing', an unusual type of singing made by making noises in the throat. It is really interesting. In fact people in the area also speak Tuvan, a type of Russian, but the language is beginning to disappear and most people there also speak Russian. Now if you look here you can see some traditional Tuvan clothes too …

4

'helo- sut wyt ti?' Now isn't that beautiful? But if you don't understand what I said, may be you should think about taking Welsh lessons! Since 1996 Welsh, once a language in danger, has become popular again. 20% of us who live in Wales now speak it! So if you aren't one of us, why not learn? Lessons are fun, cheap and easy to arrange. Then you too can sound wonderful! So come on, don't delay, get in touch today. You can email us at info@learningwelsh.co.uk or call on 0778 93485. Hwyl fawr! Goodbye!

🔊 5.4

Teacher: In today's seminar we will be looking at communication. Last week we talked about languages and how people learn them. In today's session we are going to find out more about a different way of communicating, but I'd like to start by introducing you to a guest. This is Lana, everyone, and this is Filiz, who will be translating what Lana says.

Filiz: Hi everyone. Nice to meet you. That's from both of us!

Teacher: So as you can see, Lana is using sign language. She is going to tell you more about this and her background.

Filiz: Ok. I was born deaf so I have never been able to hear anything. I can understand when people speak but I have never learnt to speak as it is very difficult for people who have been deaf since they were born. Often if a deaf person is able to hear when they grow up they learn to speak. But it is less typical for someone who has never heard anything.

I use Jordanian sign language because I was born there but I can also use American sign language too.

Student 1: Can I ask a question?

Teacher: Yes of course. Just speak clearly so that Lana can see you.

Student 1: Are there different sign languages in every country?

Filiz: Yes. Anywhere that deaf people live there are different languages in the same way that there are different spoken languages. And sometimes families have their own way of communicating and this is called 'home language'. Home languages are not recognized and usually children have to learn a formal sign language later.

Student 2: How did you learn to use sign language?

Filiz: I didn't learn really. I mean I don't remember learning. Can you all remember learning to speak? Probably not too well. And deaf children pick up sign language in the same way.

Student 1: Can you show us some of the signs you use?

Filiz: Yes of course...let me show you how to say 'happy' in American sign language. Watch...Let's do it again slowly... So, first of all, put your hand in front of you with your palm up. Next, put your little finger near your chest and make sure your thumb is away from you. Then move your hand up towards your chin in a quick movement. It should look like you are going to pat yourself under the chin. Do it a few times quickly. This means you are happy! Now you all try...

🔊 5.5

So, first of all, put your hand in front of you with your palm up. Next, put your little finger near your chest and make sure your thumb is away from you. Then move your hand up towards your chin in a quick movement. It should look like you are going to pat yourself under the chin. Do it a few times quickly. This means you are happy! Now you all try...

UNIT 6

▶ Rain and the water cycle

Heat from the sun changes water from rivers, lakes and the sea to a gas. It goes up into the sky and then turns into a liquid to make clouds. The water in the clouds later falls as rain, ice or snow.

Most of that water goes back to the rivers, lakes and sea. This is called the water cycle and it is very important. 300 million litres of water fall from the sky every day.

However, in some places in the world, rain does not fall very often. But people need rain to grow food and to drink.

So, how do we make rain when it doesn't rain? First, we need to think about how clouds become rain. Clouds are made up of small drops, or droplets of water. When the droplets get bigger they fall as rain, ice or snow. However, droplets of rain can only fall if there is some dust in the air for the water droplet to join to. The dust makes the droplet heavy enough to fall from the sky.

In one part of Texas, in the United States, this hasn't happened for a long time. There has been no rain. Gary Walker is a pilot with a very special job. He makes rain!

Gary does something called 'cloud seeding.' This means that he puts a chemical into the clouds for water to join with to make rain. Gary attaches something called silver iodide on the plane. He flies 5,486 metres up in the air. He shoots the silver iodide into the cloud. If everything goes well, rain should fall after 45 minutes. You can see more clouds in the sky. There has been 12 percent more rain from the clouds that Gary has put silver iodide into. Gary will go back into the clouds again and again to try to make more rain.

🔊 6.1

Presenter: Global warming is an important issue around the world and recently it has created more problems, this time in the Western Ghats rainforests of India. Forests are an important key to slowing down global warming because of the work that trees do for us. Trees are global cleaners: they absorb carbon dioxide, the gas which heats the atmosphere. So every time we cut down trees we are adding to the problem of climate change. And climate change then damages the forests even more, making even more trees disappear, because the changes in temperature stop the normal growth of the forest. There is now less rainfall in the rainforests which is completely changing the way they work.

Governments are beginning to work on the problem. Although they say they will stop the damage to forests, scientists don't think this is happening quickly enough. The scientists say the evidence is in the forests themselves where the types of food, the wildlife and the vegetation that animals need, are changing. In fact they believe 45% of the forest areas will have changed completely in the next 80 years.

And this is where nasikabatrachus sahyadrensis, otherwise known as the purple frog, becomes important. A report tells us that the frog is in danger of disappearing forever. One of the most unusual animals in the world, the frog can run very fast and makes a noise like a small chicken. Of course, for some people, the end of one type of frog is not important. But it is for Biju Das, a researcher from Delhi University who discovered it in 2003. For him the problems of the purple frog are evidence of what global warming is doing to the Indian rainforests. He explains that this interesting animal won't be around much longer if we don't look after the forests.

Mr Das is going to present information about the forests next week. This is when many people are meeting to talk about protecting the climate and the rainforests. According to Mr Biju, we need to plan now or we will lose some species completely. If we don't think carefully about the climate of the forests, the purple frog won't be around for much longer. On to the weather report now…

🔊 6.2

1   Did you know global warming is still increasing?
    Is it?
2   It's my birthday today.
    Really? Happy birthday.
3   The weather has got quite cold, hasn't it?
    I suppose so.
4   Thanks for inviting me to your party!
    You're welcome. It'll be nice to see you!
5   The dinner was lovely.
    Good. Glad you liked it.

🔊 6.3

Narrator: Part one

Sergio: So we need to think of some questions for this survey about the weather, Murat. Shall we just brainstorm a list of them?

Murat: I think we should decide what we want to find out. Mr Hadland told us we should look at all the different things we could survey, group them, then try to choose the most important.

Sergio: Right. Effects of weather on mood.

Murat: Well we are looking at weather in Europe where it is often cold and wet. Generally in Europe people see sunshine as positive, which I find strange. In my country, it is hot all the time so we like cooler days. But anyway… I read about some research in Germany. But it had so many different answers it wasn't clear that weather changes people's mood.

Sergio: Oh…great…

Murat: But they did find *some* specific results: they noticed that good, sunny weather didn't make people

happier. But bad weather made people more upset, if they were already unhappy.

Sergio: And…?

Murat: And, therefore, unhappy people felt even worse when it was wet and windy.

Sergio: Oh, ok. So for the 'good weather' category- no link. But for the 'bad weather' bit- it causes unhappy people to feel worse.

Murat: Yes. And the amount of sunlight seems to be linked to feeling tired. When it is sunny, people feel more energetic and less tired.

Sergio: Ok, I've added that.

Murat: Also I read something about humidity. Another experiment showed that it is more difficult to work in high humidity and, as a result, our concentration drops. And there was something about heat and anger. Really hot weather can make people angrier I think.

Sergio: Are you sure? Shall I add it?

Murat: Well write it down anyway.

Sergio: Ok, which area do you think we should look at then?

Murat: I think the humidity one is important. Especially for students.

Sergio: But the one on bad weather making people feel worse could be interesting too; it sounds like there are more useful facts with that topic.

Murat: Yes, true. I'm not sure about the very hot weather and being angry; I can't remember if that is true. So that's out. That leaves three possible topics – humidity stopping us working, or sunny weather making us less tired or bad weather making people feel worse.

Sergio: Well the one about humidity looks at how people study. It isn't really about how people feel, so it isn't useful here. I'd go with bad weather or sunny weather.

Murat: I see what you mean. We could choose either of those. I'm not sure about the bad weather one. It's a bit depressing, isn't it? Which do you prefer?

Sergio: I don't really mind.

Murat: Well if you don't mind, let's do the one about sunshine and being energetic. It's more positive.

🔊 6.4

Narrator: Part two

Murat: …and so I put all the results onto a spreadsheet on the computer. Here are all the answers from the surveys I did, 12 of them. Oh, and the three surveys that you did.

Sergio: Yes. Well … let's see what they say.

Murat: We asked about how people felt when they woke up on a sunny day.

Sergio: And?

Murat: 14 out of 15 of the people said they feel better than when it is very wet or rainy. They prefer sunshine.

Sergio: Yes.

Murat: And 13 of them said it made them feel they could get a lot of things done that day. Also 12 out of 15 people said that they did more when the weather was good.

Sergio: What about when they feel most tired?

Murat: Well everyone said that they felt tired if the weather was dull and dark. And 14 said they had most energy when there was lots of light.

Sergio: So, good weather means that people have more energy.

Murat: Well that is what our survey seems to show. Of course it might be different in another country. Maybe it depends on the place you live...

🔊 **6.5**

1 It is more difficult to work in high humidity so our concentration drops.

2 People feel more energetic in sunny weather. Therefore they can get a lot of things done if the sun is shining.

3 Some countries are very hot and don't get much rain. As a result, there isn't enough water for plants, drinking and washing.

🔊 **6.6**

1 so

2 therefore

3 as a result

UNIT 7

▶ The Palio horse race

Siena is in Tuscany, in the northwest of Italy. The city is well-known for its beautiful old buildings and its main square. It is also famous for the Palio di Siena: the most famous horse race in Italy, which takes place on 2nd July and 16th August each year.

Alberto is an Italian jockey. He practises all year for the race. The race is only three laps and takes 90 seconds. Only ten jockeys are allowed to ride in the race. Each year 50 jockeys from all over Italy try to be one of the ten.

Each jockey races for a different neighbourhood in the city. The winning neighbourhood receives the Palio: a banner which the race is named after.

One horse is chosen for each neighbourhood, using a lottery. It is only after the lottery that the neighbourhood will decide which jockey they will use in the race. Will Alberto ride in the race?

Alberto gets a phone call. The small neighbourhood of Lupa wants him to ride for them. Alberto is very happy because Lupa is where he was born.

The day of the race has come. Everyone is going to the main square. Many of them wear the colours of their neighbourhood. 60,000 people fill the square.

The jockeys enter the square. Alberto Ricceri's horse is called Zodiac. Alberto has won the race before. Can he win it now for his neighbourhood?

The Palio is a very dangerous race. The crowd is excited, but also worried.

On the second lap a jockey falls in front of Alberto's horse. There is nothing he can do. He falls too.

The race is won by the Bruco neighbourhood. Winning the Palio is everything.

Alberto wasn't hurt in the fall. Zodiac is also OK.

Everyone in his Lupa neighbourhood is very sad that they didn't win. But tomorrow, the people of Siena will start making plans for the next Palio.

🔊 **7.1**

Moderator: ...so this is our panel. In summary, Nam Ki Gan, former Taekwondo International Champion, Raina Akintola, Head of the Referees' Association and Sunan Wattana, Managing Director of Sports Technology Limited. I am moderating so I will be asking for questions. And our first question is about scoring.

Audience: Yes. Can I ask what you think about the new scoring system for this competition? Is it a good idea or not?

Moderator: Are you talking about the sensor vest?

Audience: Yes.

Moderator: Ok. For those of you who don't know about this, for the first time, the vest will be used to help with scores in the competition. I've brought one here to show you. Have a look. It's going to change the way we check the scoring. As you probably know, in Taekwondo, competitors can win points by kicking or hitting the other person. The new vest has sensors in it: little computer chips that know if there is a hit or kick. Here you can see one. The sensors can tell if there is a strong kick or hit and count the points. So, let's start with Sunan Wattana, Managing Director of Sports Technology Limited. Sunan...

Sunan: Yes, of course the new system is a good idea. Obviously scoring was causing a lot of problems before.

Moderator: What do you mean?

Sunan: Well, in many of the most important competitions in recent years, the scores have caused arguments because the referees have made mistakes.

Moderator: Raina, what do you think about that? Has the scoring caused problems before?

Raina: Actually the scoring has worked well compared to other sports, I don't agree. We haven't tested the new system yet so we don't know if it will work. It also doesn't work if there is a kick to the head. So it definitely isn't needed. There haven't been that many problems at all.

Moderator: Really?

Raina: No of course not.

Moderator: Nam, what's your view?

Nam Ki: Well it probably won't cause any problems if we have a new system. We can use both things: the referee and the vest. In the past, there have been times when the referee hasn't seen all the hits. And also competitors have tried to confuse them by using shouts and noises too. So computer sensors in vests will help in these situations.

Moderator: I see.

Nam Ki: Yes, I think, on balance, a vest with a computer sensor is a good idea. But it shouldn't replace the referee yet. Like Raina says, the vest hasn't been tested enough. We can't rely on it completely.

🔊 **7.2**

1 The teacher's name isn't Mr Rosso. It's Mr Rosson.

2 I took a golf lesson, not a cricket lesson.

3 The match is at six thirty tonight, not six, so don't be late.

4 She doesn't take drama, she studies sport.

5 The competition will be in Azerbaijan, not in Kyrgyzstan.

🔊 **7.3**

Yasmin: For my project I looked at some unusual sports that people play around the world. I'd like to start by talking about chess boxing. You may already know about the two sports. Chess is a game played with a board and different chess pieces. Very intelligent people often play this game because it needs players to think very carefully. Boxing is a totally different kind of sport though; being strong is more important because boxers have to hit each other. They wear gloves and helmets in the ring but it is still difficult. Now 'chess boxing' is a new type of sport where the players do both sports. They start with boxing, sorry, I mean chess, and then do some boxing and they continue doing each sport in turn. The person who wins the boxing or the chess first is the champion. One benefit of this sport is that it tests people physically and mentally. It isn't just thinking or physical activity, it is both.

Another sport which tests people is urban golf. Urban golf is similar to normal golf but you don't need to go to a golf course. You get clubs and a golf ball- well actually, it is a soft tennis ball instead of a hard golf one. Then you can play in the street, which is why it is called 'urban'. An advantage of urban golf is that you don't need to go anywhere special or need much money to play. You just agree where you want to hit the ball, for example, a sign in the street or a rubbish bin. On the other hand, you may break something if you hit the ball too hard!

Next I'd like to talk about the Morrocan desert footrace which is also called the Marathon Des Sables or the Sahara marathon. This race is held every year over a week, or rather over six days. On the longest day the runners have to travel 57 miles. The best thing about it is that the winner can say he or she has won the hardest marathon in the world.

Finally I'd like to look at Sepak Takraw. This is a type of volleyball and is very popular in Southeast Asia. The players use a different kind of ball and they can use their feet, knees, chest and head. The sport began in Indonesia and it- no not Indonesia, it began in Malaysia although it is also very popular in Thailand and Indonesia. One good thing about Sepak Takraw is that it is now played in schools in many countries including Canada and gets children doing sport.

🔊 **7.4**

1 An advantage of this is …

2 A disadvantage of this is …

3 A benefit of this is …

4 A problem with this is …

5 The best thing about this is …

6 The worst thing about this is …

7 One good thing is …

8 One bad thing is …

UNIT 8

▶ South African Cape fishermen

This is South Africa's cape peninsula – the Cape of Good Hope. The weather here is dangerous and changes quickly. Storms and the dangerous sea in this area have caused a lot of ships to sink.

David fishes here and understands these dangers very well. His father went missing when he was fishing. David never saw him again. David knows the dangers better than most people, but these waters are also a way for him to earn money.

The waters around the cape are rich in small plants and animals and are home to 2,000 different types of fish. David fishes for one of these, the Snoek: a food that is very popular in the area. The problem is that they are very difficult to find.

This is because Snoek look for food and don't stay in the same place for long.

David has a modern fishing boat but he still catches Snoek in the old way, with hand-held fishing lines. Sometimes David can wait many months before he finds any fish.

But then his luck changes! Snoek are dangerous and can bite. David teaches his sons what he learned from his father: how to catch Snoek. He says this helps to make the family strong because everyone works together. Today they find lots of Snoek. They catch over 300 fish: it's a good day!

🔊 **8.1**

1 Forty eight per cent

2 a half

3 one third

4 Thirty one point five

5 One hundred and three

6 One thousand, five hundred and forty

7 Six thousand and one

🔊 **8.2**

Prof. Gould: Shall we look at your project now?

Alika: Ok yes.

Prof. Gould: You've done a lot of reading for this, which is great. I can see you have noted a lot of information down.

Alika: Yes I haven't finished yet; I ran out of time. But I read as much as I could. About 103 different reports.

As you can see, I noted down the key information and I took part in the discussions on this with students from my seminar group. I found out a large amount of information.

Prof.Gould: Good. So you studied the way people work for your project. Can you tell me what you learnt?

Alika: Well I looked at how people spend time at work. I was interested in how people wasted time and why they didn't work hard in their job; I mean the reasons why they didn't get on with their work. I found out a lot of interesting information. For example, that almost half of the workers wasted time on the internet. They were surfing the internet or writing personal emails. It was 48% of workers in fact. 31.5% also said that they spent time talking to colleagues instead of working. And just under half that amount, 15%, said they took longer coffee and lunch breaks than they should. Just 5% said they spent time texting friends and making plans for after work.

Prof. Gould: Good. And did you find out the reasons why?

Alika: Yes. Approximately half said they didn't work hard because they weren't happy with their job.

Prof. Gould: I see.

Alika: And about a third, 33.5%, thought they didn't earn enough. They said they didn't have enough money for holidays or nice clothes. They only just had enough money to get by, so they didn't work as hard as they could. Some people said they had to work too many hours...

🔊 **8.3**

Mentor: Hi Sami. Good to see you again.

Sami: Hello.

Mentor: So, last time we met we did a practice job interview. Did you enjoy it?

Sami: Enjoy it ...? No not really. You gave me a hard time! But it was very useful.

Mentor: Oh yes? Why was it useful?

Sami: Well I realized how scary it could be!

Mentor: Exactly! But you remember some of the questions?

Sami: Yes. You asked me loads ... why would you like to work with us? What are your strengths and weaknesses? Why should we give you the job? What do you want to do long term ...

Mentor: Wow – well done!

Sami: And what else was there? Are you always on time? Are you good at working in a team? What kind of qualifications have you got? When did you last solve a difficult problem?...Is that enough?

Mentor: Well, no problems with your memory Sami! So let's think about what was good in the interview and what you could improve. I think you did a good job answering all the questions. You were very calm and you listened carefully, which is good.

Sami: Oh ok. Well that is good to know.

Mentor: You also gave lots of detail and talked about what you have done before which is great

Sami: I see.

Mentor: You have some excellent work experience so if I were you, in the next interview you have, I would also take along some examples of your work from before. You could show them what you can do.

Sami: Yeah I like that idea.

Mentor: But, there are things we can work on. If you want to do better, you should start by looking more confident and answering the questions with confidence.

You did a good job but you looked very nervous all the time. You didn't look me in the eyes at all. You looked at the table mostly.

Sami: I see. Well in my country it can be rude to look someone in the eyes.

Mentor: I understand. But I think if you are interviewed by someone in this country, you need to make eye contact. People think you are being unfriendly or nervous if you don't look at them. It isn't seen as a good thing.

Sami: Mmm ... I will try. Someone else told me this but sometimes I forget the difference in culture.

Mentor: Yes. It is easy to forget things like this when we are nervous. Look up at the person speaking to you and speak with confidence. Also you should think about your clothes. You don't look ... well, you could be smarter.

Sami: I see. I'll try.

🔊 **8.4**

Mentor: Hi Sami. Good to see you again.

Sami: Hello.

Mentor: So, last time we met we did a practice job interview. Did you enjoy it?

Sami: Enjoy it ...? No not really. You gave me a hard time! But it was very useful.

Mentor: Oh yes? Why was it useful?

Sami: Well I realized how scary it could be!

Mentor: Exactly! But you remember some of the questions?

Sami: Yes. You asked me loads ... why would you like to work with us? What are your strengths and weaknesses? Why should we give you the job? What do you want to do long term ...

Mentor: Wow- well done!

🔊 **8.5**

e   Oh yes?

🔊 **8.6**

b   Enjoy it? No not really.

c   Did you enjoy it?

e   Oh yes?

UNIT 9

🔵 Internet inventors

Narrator: The internet has become part of our daily lives. We use it for work, to talk with friends, to buy things and to find out information. But, do you ever think about who invented the world wide web and who started the websites that you use every day?

They all came from one person's good idea. The British computer scientist Sir Tim Berners-Lee invented the world wide web in 1989. He wanted it to be free for everyone to use. He didn't want it to be a place for big businesses. The web is now a place where we can all speak and be listened to.

In the past, big book, film and music companies decided what we read, watched and listened to. We often had to spend a lot of money to get what we wanted.

But that has changed. Websites like Craigslist™ and Wikipedia™ show what can be done for free.

In the old days you had to pay to put advertisements in the newspaper. On Craigslist™, you don't have to pay a thing. You can find jobs and houses, sell a computer or buy a car. All for free. Craig Newmark started Craigslist™ in 1996 and runs it from a small office in San Francisco. It is now a free online noticeboard in 50 countries around the world.

Craig Newmark is not the only one building an online community. Jimmy Wales started Wikipedia™. Wikipedia™ is an encyclopaedia that anyone can write for.

It was started in 2001 and is available in 285 languages. It has 100 times more information than in old, paper encyclopaedias, but anyone can change pages on the site. It means that new information is added as soon as things happen.

So, next time you talk to your friends, buy, or sell something online, think about how one good idea can change people's daily lives.

🔊 9.1

Yasmin: Hello.

Sam: Hi, is that Yasmin? It's Sam here.

Yasmin: Hi Sam! How are you?

Sam: OK I suppose. I'm not that great.

Yasmin: Oh dear, what's up? Are you bored?

Sam: It's the history essay. You know, the one on remarkable people in the past who have done something really interesting or unusual. I'm not finding it very easy to write. Have you done it yet?

Yasmin: Yes I have. I've just got to write a conclusion.

Sam: Good for you. I bet it's really good.

Yasmin: Thanks Sam. I'm quite pleased with it, but the introduction's not great. It needs a bit more work. How much have you written?

Sam: Well ... I haven't done all of it ...

Yasmin: All or any of it?

Sam: I'm not very good at finding things to write about. I'm having trouble thinking of any ideas. Who did you do yours on?

Yasmin: I did Joshua Abraham Norton. He was a fascinating man.

Sam: Who's he? What did he do?

Yasmin: Well his early life was very normal. He grew up in South Africa and had a business there but it didn't work. So then he went to America in 1849 because he thought he could get rich.

Sam: And was he right?

Yasmin: Well to start with he was quite successful. But then his business failed and he lost all his money in 1853. He became homeless and started living in the streets. I think he went a bit mad.

Sam: That's sad. But his life doesn't sound that extraordinary. Why are you interested in him?

Yasmin: The unusual bit was in 1859. He declared to everyone in San Francisco that he was the President of America and he started to walk around the streets in a uniform with a big hat and a sword. He became quite famous. The people around him called him 'emperor'

and when the police tried to arrest him people were very angry and he was let free again. He even made his own paper money and the shops would let him use it. When he died in 1880 he was still homeless but thirty thousand people came to his funeral.

Sam: That is amazing! Wow... I need to find someone like that.

Yasmin: Why don't you do something on Joseph Conrad? Do you know about him?

Sam: Erm ... I don't know a lot about Conrad ... who ...

Yasmin: He was a Polish writer. But he didn't write in Polish, he wrote in English. I think he was a sailor before he became a writer, but you'd need to check that.

Sam: Ok ... I will have a look.

Yasmin: Do you know what the teacher wants us to write?

Sam: Well I'm not sure I understand everything...

🔊 9.2

1 I'm quite pleased with it.
2 He was a fascinating man.
3 That is amazing!
4 I will have a look.

🔊 9.3

Teacher: Hello everyone. So in this seminar we're going to look at the design of some everyday objects: things that we see or use every day and that we often don't think about. I asked you to look at some pictures for homework. Actually these objects are often simple things that have changed our lives. For example, matches used for starting fires, rucksacks to carry things easily, lamps for studying at night, even headphones. All these are things we don't notice at all but they were all designed once.

Lara: Yes. Like a belt for example. How was that designed? Or a broom? Or what about a chair?

Teacher: Exactly. Chairs are actually a good example. Think about the egg chair which we looked at before. It was designed by Arne Jacobsen in 1958.

Razia: I remember that. It is kind of round, isn't it? In lots of lovely, different colours. It's a beautiful design but it's probably not very comfortable.

Teacher: You could be right. So today we are going to think about these design issues. First of all, I will show you some objects and their uses, look at what makes them special and what they are made of. And we can think about the advantages or disadvantages they have. So, moving on, let's look at this first picture: a wheelbarrow.

Ebru: Oh that is a really nice design. What's it made of?

Razia: It's made of plastic I think. And maybe some metal.

Teacher: Yes. But let's start by thinking about how it is used: the most important thing to consider in design. In fact you can tell me, what's it used for?

Ebru: Isn't it used for moving things around the garden, such as plants or earth?

Teacher: Yes, which this wheel barrow could easily do. But in design we also need to ask 'What does it look like?' So, how many parts does it have?

Lara: Well it has two parts, the square frame used to carry things and the circular wheel. But it's a special wheel: it is completely round. I guess this is so that the wheelbarrow can move more easily. The design is unusual.

Razia: And I agree the advantage is that it is much easier to carry things and move with this wheelbarrow.

Teacher: Yes. But can you think of any disadvantages?

Lara: I am sure it is expensive compared to other wheelbarrows!

Teacher: It can be. The man who invented it, James Dyson, is very rich now. But he became famous because of the interesting shapes he uses in his design work. In fact who would like to present the second picture of his work?

Lara: I can. I read about this. So, let's look at the second example of a Dyson design. It's a hand-dryer. Possibly you have used one to dry your hands in a public bathroom. It is made from one big single part so it looks very basic. Can you see that it is long and rectangular from the front? But if you look closely you can see a circular space where we can put our hands to dry. It is a beautiful design because it saves time – you can dry your hands quickly without using towels or paper or touching buttons. Finally though, I can say that there is a disadvantage – if the electricity is cut then you can't use it!

Ebru: Oh I have a picture of another object which doesn't have the electricity problem because it runs on batteries. It is a car with a special design. It was designed by Roman Mistiuk for Peugeot and it's called the Metromorph. It's really extraordinary. Look, here's a picture. As you can see, it's oval-shaped and its sides and roof are made of plastic or glass.

Ebru: What's so special about it?

Razia: Well it is designed to save space in the future. Drivers won't have to find a parking space in our busy cities with the Metromorph because it will be able to climb up the outside of the building to an apartment and 'park' outside.

Ebru: Wow! That's amazing! But we won't all live in very modern high-rise flats though, will we?

Razia: You're right. It won't be able to climb all types of building. But it might solve some of our space problems. Also, it's not just a climbing car. It's also a balcony! Look. You can see through the sides and the roof of the car.

Ebru: Oh yes!

Razia: Well, that means that people can stand in the car when it's parked and look out over the city.

Ebru: Wow. A car with a view ...

🔊 **9.4**

1a What's it made of?
b It's made of plastic and metal.
2a What's it used for?
b It's used for playing a radio without electricity.
3a What is this thing used for?
b It's a thing used for winding the radio up.
4a What is this part used to do?
b It's used to do the winding

UNIT 10

▶ Exploring Mars

People have already been to the moon. Will we one day go to Mars? Mars was one of the first planets that was seen through a telescope. A spacecraft was sent to take pictures of Mars in 1964. Before this, some astronomers believed that there might be life on the planet. They were wrong, but NASA didn't stop looking.

Spacecraft sent to Mars since 2000 have found that there might be ice on the planet. In 2002, the Odyssey spacecraft took pictures of Mars, using a special instrument that could see the details of the light from space. It found that there could be ice on Mars.

Other pictures show us that there might have been old lakes and rivers. Was there once life on Mars? On August 4th, 2007, The Phoenix Mars Lander was sent into space. It finally arrived on Mars on May 25th, 2008. Phoenix's job was to study the history of water on the planet. Phoenix was digging the soil on Mars. It found ice about one metre down. The ice that the spacecraft had shown was there.

Phoenix spent five months sending important information to NASA. It was the first spacecraft sent to Mars that found water on the planet. Phoenix last sent a message to NASA in November 2008, but that was not the end.

The Curiosity Rover arrived on Mars on August 6th 2012. It is looking for life. Curiosity has enough batteries to look at Mars for ten years. What will it find?

🔊 **10.1**

1 When the sun is out, I make sure my son uses cream so he isn't burnt.
2 Have you read the information about the red planet?
3 We are having a picnic whether it is hot or not. It has been good weather recently so we are hoping it will be nice.
4 She ate her dinner before she went out at eight o'clock.
5 There are two doctors in the family and their daughter is also studying medicine.
6 Our visitor was in the house for an hour.

🔊 **10.2**

1 It is very nice weather today.
2 I waited for an hour.
3 Are you going there later?
4 I read the book yesterday.
5 We ate our dinner.
6 I don't mind.

🔊 **10.3**

Narrator: Part 1

Presenter: In this episode of *Astronomy Today* we are looking at space travel and the journeys that people hope to make beyond the moon. We'll think about the planets people haven't visited yet and whether we are likely to tour some of them in the future. Let's begin inside our own solar system. If someone asked you the name of a famous planet, you would probably say Venus, Mars, Neptune or even the sun.

But the one scientists hope to visit next is Mars. Mars is known as the Red Planet because of its colour – and there are now plans to send two people to visit it. An organisation called Inspiration Mars hopes to send the carefully selected people to Mars in the next few years.

🔊 10.4

Narrator: Part 2

Presenter: Inspiration Mars wants to send a husband and wife on the voyage. If they can find a married couple who have the right experience, they believe the couple will be able to help each other on the journey which will take 501 days and is very dangerous. The spacecraft won't be able to land on the surface of Mars but it will travel around the planet to get information. Despite the danger, thousands of people have sent letters to Inspiration Mars because they want to go. Inspiration Mars hope the trip will be possible in the next four years.

Outside our solar system there is another planet more surprising than Mars and many people would go there if we had the technology to send them. It is called Lucy and is bigger than the Earth. But the most surprising fact is that this planet is a huge diamond. Scientists have always known about the diamond planets created from heat. They are all outside our own solar system like Lucy. Lucy is about 4000 kilometres across, twice as wide as the Earth and eight times as heavy. It turns so fast that one year passes in 18 hours. If this planet were mined, there would be more diamonds found on it than all the diamonds on Earth through history. But the planet is hot- it has a temperature of 3500 degrees and is probably going to burn up soon. And while the trip to explore Mars is planned for the next few years, scientists have not found a way to travel outside our own solar system yet. Perhaps one day.

🔊 10.5

1a tree   b three
2a tank   b thank
3a bat   b bath
4a true   b through

🔊 10.6

Narrator: Part 1

Presenter: Hello everyone. We'll begin today's discussion with a look at space exploration. This is controlled from the International Space Station. We'll think about what type of work the space station does and whether the money we spend is worth it. We will then look at the future of the station. I have with me Dorota Loy, an engineer from the Space Development Project, Raj Padow, researcher in Environmental Studies and Chen Wu who is a professor of Astrophysics. Let me ask Chen to start us off by giving us some more information about the space station.

🔊 10.7

Narrator: Part 2

Chen: Well, the space station is where we do research and get information about many things. The scientists on the station do experiments and learn about Biology, Physics and space environment for example. And for me, the most important thing is that they are finding out more about future space travel.

Dorota: Yes, I agree the space station is used for a lot of scientific study.

Chen: It isn't cheap to run but the money we spend is definitely worth it. The truth is, we couldn't do the same research without it. The work on the Space Station has shown us many things about how space works, what stars do, the effects on people who stay in space for a long time and so on. We must continue to do this work so that we can explore space further away and –...

Raj: Can I just say something here? I agree with Chen that we need the space station. But even he says it is very expensive. I know that we have to spend money to develop. But for me, the most important reason is that we are using it to learn about the earth and what is happening to our planet. We have people in the world who don't have enough food or housing. If we are exploring space, we should think about how this can help us on Planet Earth. For me this is the main reason we-

Chen: Space exploration is vital though. It is-

Raj: Sorry, Chen, can I finish my point? If we are going to spend so much money on the Space Station, the most important thing we should be doing is finding out more about the environment on Earth. There is no point finding new planets when we don't look after our own!

Presenter: Dorota, you haven't said much so far. Any thoughts?

Dorota: Well I personally don't see a problem. Chen is talking about space travel and Raj about improving life on Earth. But we can do both these things – learn more about the Earth and also about space. We have learnt a huge amount about the planets and space travel but we have also learnt about –

Chen: Yes exactly – space travel...

Dorota: Please allow me to finish. We have also learnt about geographic and environment change and this information could not have been found any other way. I think in the future we can continue to use the Space Station to develop both.

Presenter: Professor Chen, Raj Padow, let's get your thoughts on this. Do you think this is true?

Chen: Of course. Dorota is absolutely right.

Raj: And I agree too. But as I said, only if the money spent helps us on our own planet too.

Presenter: Ok, so some agreement here then. Let's go back to the idea of space travel and think about that first of all. So does anybody want to...

ACKNOWLEDGEMENTS

Author acknowledgements

I would like to acknowledge the invaluable patience and professionalism of Verity, Kate, Caroline and the editing team at CUP. Special mention to my students, old and new, who are always inspirational, and to Francoise, Anna and Lindsay for being wonderful colleagues and friends. Finally thanks to Ata and my parents for all the important stuff.
Stephanie Dimond-Bayir

Publisher acknowledgements

The publishers are extremely grateful to the following people and their students for reviewing and trialling this course during its development. The course has benefited hugely from your insightful comments and feedback.

Mr M.K. Adjibade, King Saud University, Saudi Arabia; Canan Aktug, Bursa Technical University, Turkey; Olwyn Alexander, Heriot Watt University, UK; Valerie Anisy, Damman University, Saudi Arabia; Anwar Al-Fetlawi, University of Sharjah, UAE; Laila Al-Qadhi, Kuwait University, Kuwait; Tahani Al-Taha, University of Dubai, UAE; Ozlem Atalay, Middle East Technical University, Turkey; Seda Merter Ataygul, Bursa Technical University Turkey; Harika Altug, Bogazici University, Turkey; Kwab Asare, University of Westminster, UK; Erdogan Bada, Cukurova University, Turkey; Cem Balcikanli, Gazi University, Turkey; Gaye Bayri, Anadolu University, Turkey; Meher Ben Lakhdar, Sohar University, Oman; Emma Biss, Girne American University, UK; Dogan Bulut, Meliksah University, Turkey; Sinem Bur, TED University, Turkey; Alison Chisholm, University of Sussex, UK; Dr. Panidnad Chulerk , Rangsit University, Thailand; Sedat Cilingir, Bilgi University, Istanbul, Turkey; Sarah Clark, Nottingham Trent International College, UK; Elaine Cockerham, Higher College of Technology, Muscat, Oman; Asli Derin, Bilgi University, Turkey; Steven Douglass, University of Sunderland, UK; Jacqueline Einer, Sabanci University, Turkey; Basak Erel, Anadolu University, Turkey; Hande Lena Erol, Piri Reis Maritime University, Turkey; Gulseren Eyuboglu, Ozyegin University, Turkey; Muge Gencer, Kemerburgaz University, Turkey; Dr. Majid Gharawi and colleagues at the English Language Centre, Jazan University, Saudi Arabia; Jeff Gibbons, King Fahed University of Petroleum and Minerals, Saudi Arabia; Maxine Gilway, Bristol University, UK; Dr Christina Gitsaki, HCT, Dubai Men's College, UAE; Sam Fenwick, Sohar University, Oman; Peter Frey, International House, Doha, Qatar; Neil Harris, Swansea University, UK; Vicki Hayden, College of the North Atlantic, Qatar; Ajarn Naratip Sharp Jindapitak, Prince of Songkla University, Hatyai, Thailand; Joud Jabri-Pickett, United Arab Emirates University, Al Ain, UAE; Aysel Kilic, Anadolu University, Turkey; Ali Kimav, Anadolu University, Turkey; Bahar Kiziltunali, Izmir University of Economics, Turkey; Kamil Koc, Ozel Kasimoglu Coskun Lisesi, Turkey; Ipek Korman-Tezcan, Yeditepe University, Turkey; Philip Lodge, Dubai Men's College, UAE; Iain Mackie, Al Rowdah University, Abu Dhabi, UAE; Katherine Mansfield, University of Westminster, UK; Kassim Mastan, King Saud University, Saudi Arabia; Elspeth McConnell, Newham College, UK; Lauriel Mehdi, American University of Sharjah, UAE; Dorando Mirkin-Dick, Bell International Institute, UK; Dr Sita Musigrungsi, Prince of Songkla University, Hatyai, Thailand; Mark Neville, Al Hosn University, Abu Dhabi, UAE; Shirley Norton, London School of English, UK; James Openshaw, British Study Centres, UK; Hale Ottolini, Mugla Sitki Kocman University, Turkey; David Palmer, University of Dubai, UAE; Michael Pazinas, United Arab Emirates University, UAE; Troy Priest, Zayed University, UAE; Alison Ramage Patterson, Jeddah, Saudi Arabia; Paul Rogers, Study Skills Academy, Qatar; Josh Round, Saint George International, UK; Harika Saglicak, Bogazici University, Turkey; Asli Saracoglu, Isik University, Turkey; Neil Sarkar, Ealing, Hammersmith and West London College, UK; Nancy Shepherd, Bahrain University, Bahrain; Jonathan Smith, Sabanci University, Turkey; Peter Smith, United Arab Emirates University, UAE; Adem Soruc, Fatih University Istanbul, Turkey; Dr Peter Stanfield, HCT, Madinat Zayed & Ruwais Colleges, UAE; Maria Agata Szczerbik, United Arab Emirates University, Al Ain, UAE; Burcu Tezcan-Unal, Bilgi University, Turkey; Dr Nakonthep Tipayasuparat, Rangsit University, Thailand; Scott Thornbury, The New School, New York, USA; Susan Toth, HCT, Dubai Men's Campus, Dubai, UAE; Melin Unal, Ege University, Izmir, Turkey; Aylin Unaldi, Bogaziçi University, Turkey; Colleen Wackrow, Princess Nourah bint Abdulrahman University, Riyadh, Saudi Arabia; Gordon Watts, Study Group, Brighton UK; Po Leng Wendelkin, INTO at University of East Anglia, UK; Halime Yildiz, Bilkent University, Ankara, Turkey; Ferhat Yilmaz, Kahramanmaras Sutcu Imam University, Turkey.

Special thanks to Peter Lucantoni for sharing his expertise, both pedagogical and cultural.

Text and Photo acknowledgements

The authors and publishers acknowledge the following sources of copyright material and are grateful for the permissions granted. While every effort has been made, it has not always been possible to identify the sources of all the material used, or to trace all copyright holders. If any omissions are brought to our notice, we will be happy to include the appropriate acknowledgements on reprinting.

p.12:(1) © Eric Limon/Shutterstock; p.12: (2) © szefei/Shutterstock; p.12: (3) © Steven Vidler/Eurasia Press/Corbis; pp.14/15: ©A Demotes/Getty Images; p.18 & 26(a): © Walter Bibikow/Getty Images; p.18 & 26(b): © Heracles Kritikos/Shutterstock; p.18 & 26(c): © Massimo Pizzotti/Getty Images; p.18 & 26(d): Hulton Archive/Getty Images; p.23 © Pincasso/Shutterstock; pp.32/33: © Floris Leeuwenberg/Corbis; p.34(BC): AFP/Getty Images; p.36(L): Redferns/Getty Images; p.36(C): © Max Derets/Getty Images; p.36(R): © Thomas Imo/Alamy; p.42(a): © James Davies; p.42(b): Photo Cuisine/Alamy; p.42(c): © David Muir/Getty Images; p.42(d): Wiz Data Inc/Alamy; p.44(L): Naturesports/Shutterstock; p.44(R): Bloomberg/Getty Images; p.46(T): Imagemore.Co.Ltd/Corbis; p.46(CR): © Derek Mallan/Travelink/Corbis; p.46(BR): © Michael Coyne/Getty Images; p.46(B): AFP/Getty Images; p.47(C): © Simon Reddy/Alamy; p.47(B): Travelbild.com/Alamy; pp.50/51: AFP/Getty Images; p.59: © wavebreakmedia/Shutterstock; p.60(TL): © Kzenon/Alamy; p.60(TC): © Ariel Skelley/Blend Images/Getty Images; p.60(TR): Echo/Getty Images; p.64(1): Tao Associates/Getty Images; p.64(2): Caro/Alamy; p.64(3): © Jenny Norquist/Moodboard/Alamy; p.64(4): © Sami Sarkis/Getty Images; p.64(5): Jupiter Images/Getty Images; pp.68/69: © Andrew Brookes/Corbis; p.72(1): © Sam Toren/Alamy; p.72(2): Disability Images/Alamy; p.72(3): © Howard Kingsnorth/Getty Images; p.72(4): © Kevin Schafer/Getty Images; p.72(5): Moodboard/Alamy; p.78: Hero Images/Corbis; pp.86/87: RG Images/Stock4B/Corbis; p.92: © Alok Das/Survival International; p.95: © Janine Wiedel Photo Library/Alamy; p.98: © Christophe Dernbach/epa/Corbis; pp.104/105: © Hercules Milas/Alamy; p.106: dieKleinert/Alamy; p.108: © James Davies; p.109(L): © Rolando Gil/Getty Images; p.109(C): © Richard Packwood/Getty Images; p.109(R): © Adrees Latif/Reuters; p.115: © Eric Audras/Getty Images; p.122/123: Getty Images; p.126: © Simon Balson/Alamy; p.132(1): Getty Images; p.132(2): AFP/Getty Images; p.132(3): © Nicky Loh/Getty Images; p.132(4): © Soren Stache/epa/Corbis; p.135: © Emma Wood/Alamy; pp.140/141: Bloomberg/Getty Images; p.150: © Jack Hollingsworth/Corbis; pp.158/159: © Jack Sullivan/Alamy; p.162: Bettmann/Corbis; p.166: Hulton Archive/Getty Images; p.168(1): © Benjamin Stansall/Alamy; p.168(2): Rex Features; p.168(3): © James Davies; p.168(4): Arcaid Images/Alamy; p.170: © John Joannides/Alamy; p.173(match): © Dennis Nata/Shutterstock; p.173(lamp): © Mary981/Shutterstock; p.173(bucket): © Andrey Eremin/Shutterstock; p.173(mug): Instudios.me/Shutterstock; p.173(comb): © Winai Tepsuttinun/Shutterstock; p.173(rucksack): Gresei/Shutterstock; p.173(ruler): Smile Studio/Shutterstock; p.173(belt): © Popkov Nikolay/Shutterstock; p.173(broom): Jarp2/Shutterstock; p.173(headphones): © Alexander Demyanenko/Shutterstock; pp.176/177: © Babak Tafreshi/Twan/Science Photo Library; p.178: US Geological Survey/Science Photo Library; p.181: © Travis Metcalfe and Ruth Bazinet, Harvard-Smithsonian Center for Astrophysics; p.186: Getty Images; p.194: © David Bagnall/Alamy; p.195(1) Raywoo/Alamy; p.195(2): © Finbarr Webster/Alamy; p.196: © Michelle Falzone/Alamy; p.198(L): Raywoo/Alamy; p.198(R): © Finbarr Webster/Alamy.

Diagram on p. 172 used with kind permission of Freeplay Energy Ltd.

All video stills by kind permission of © Discovery Communication, LLC 2014

Illustrations

Clive Goodyer p.154; Fiona Gowen p.22; Ben Hasler p.96; Bob Lea p.187; Oxford Designers & Illustrators pp.47, 55, 100, 119, 142, 197.

Dictionary

Cambridge dictionaries are the world's most widely used dictionaries for learners of English. Available at three levels (Cambridge Essential English Dictionary, Cambridge Learner's Dictionary and Cambridge Advanced Learner's Dictionary), they provide easy-to-understand definitions, example sentences, and help in avoiding typical mistakes. The dictionaries are also available online at dictionary.cambridge.org. © Cambridge University Press, reproduced with permission.

Corpus

Development of this publication has made use of the Cambridge English Corpus (CEC). The CEC is a multi-billion word computer database of contemporary spoken and written English. It includes British English, American English and other varieties of English. It also includes the Cambridge Learner Corpus, developed in collaboration with Cambridge English Language Assessment. Cambridge University Press has built up the CEC to provide evidence about language use that helps to produce better language teaching materials.

Picture research by Alison Prior.

Typeset by emc design ltd.